Word Tracing

A is for

antelope

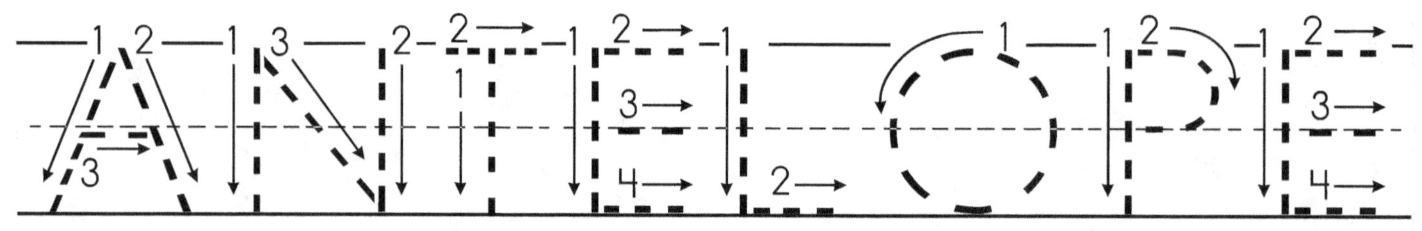

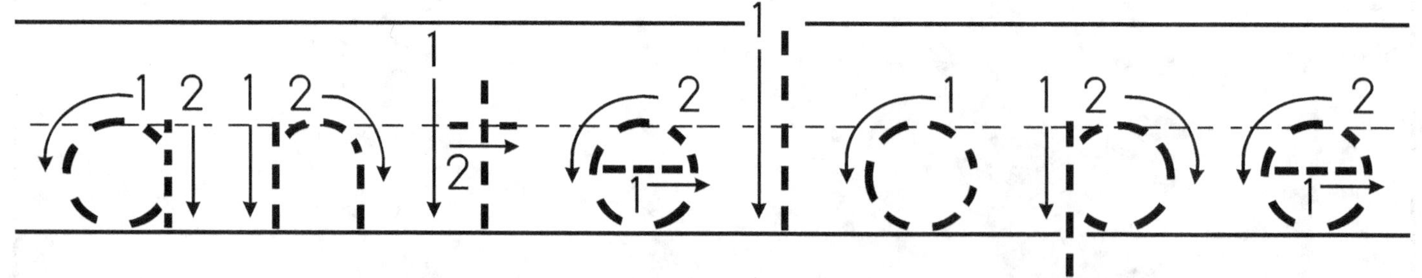

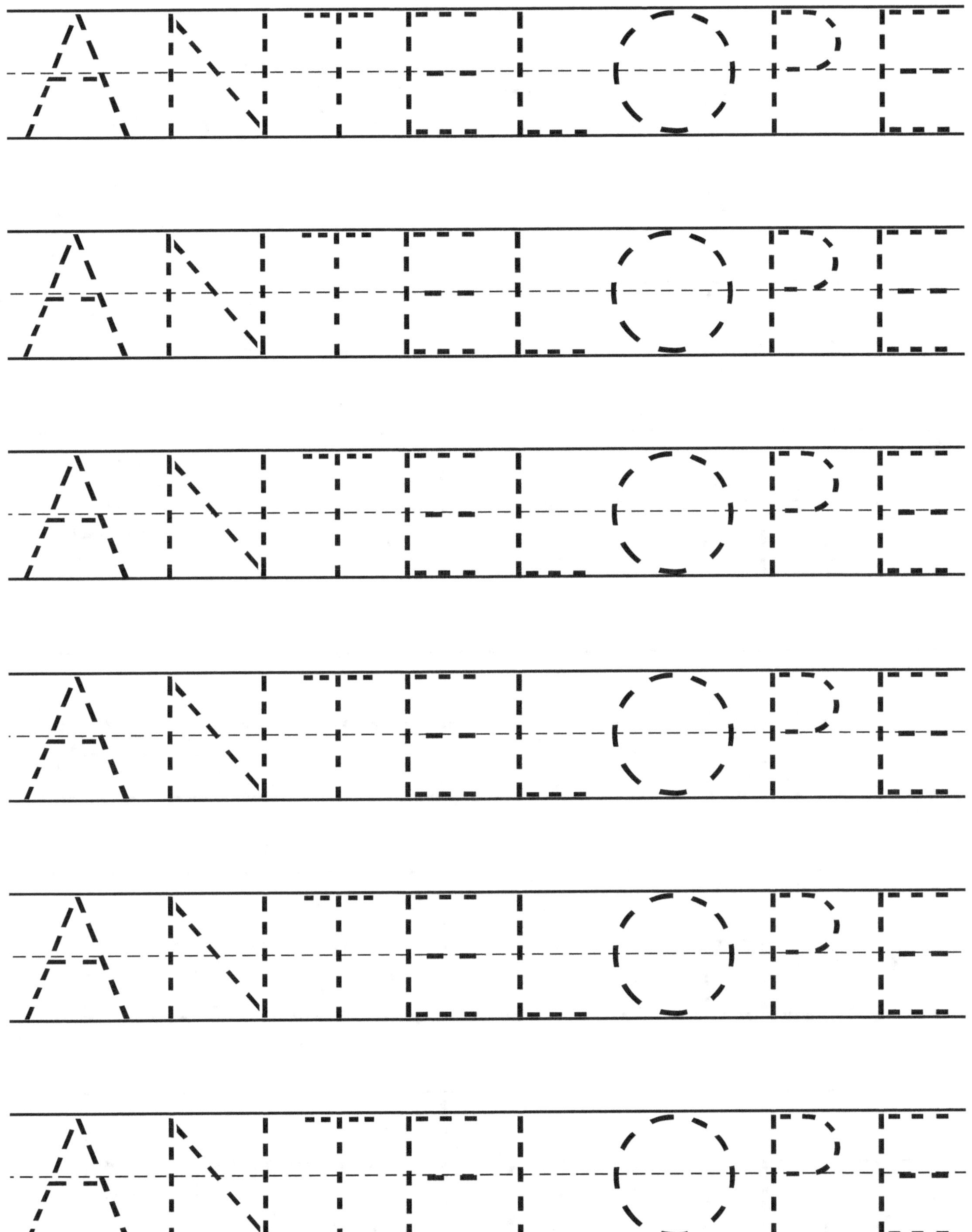

antelope

antelope

antelope

antelope

antelope

antelope

B is for

bear

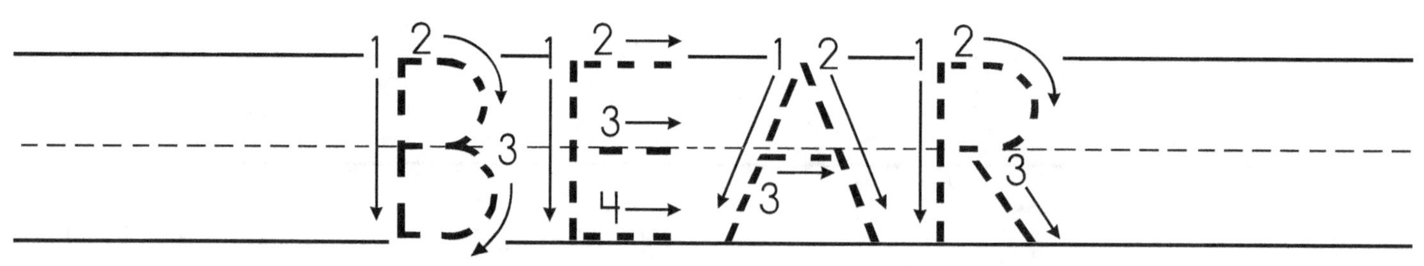

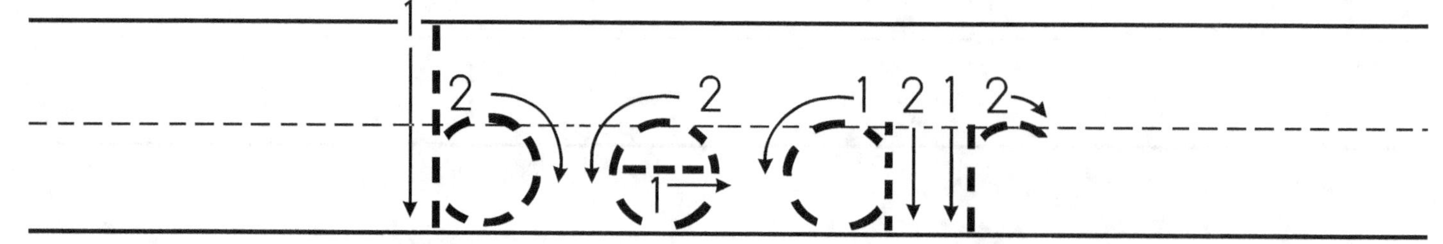

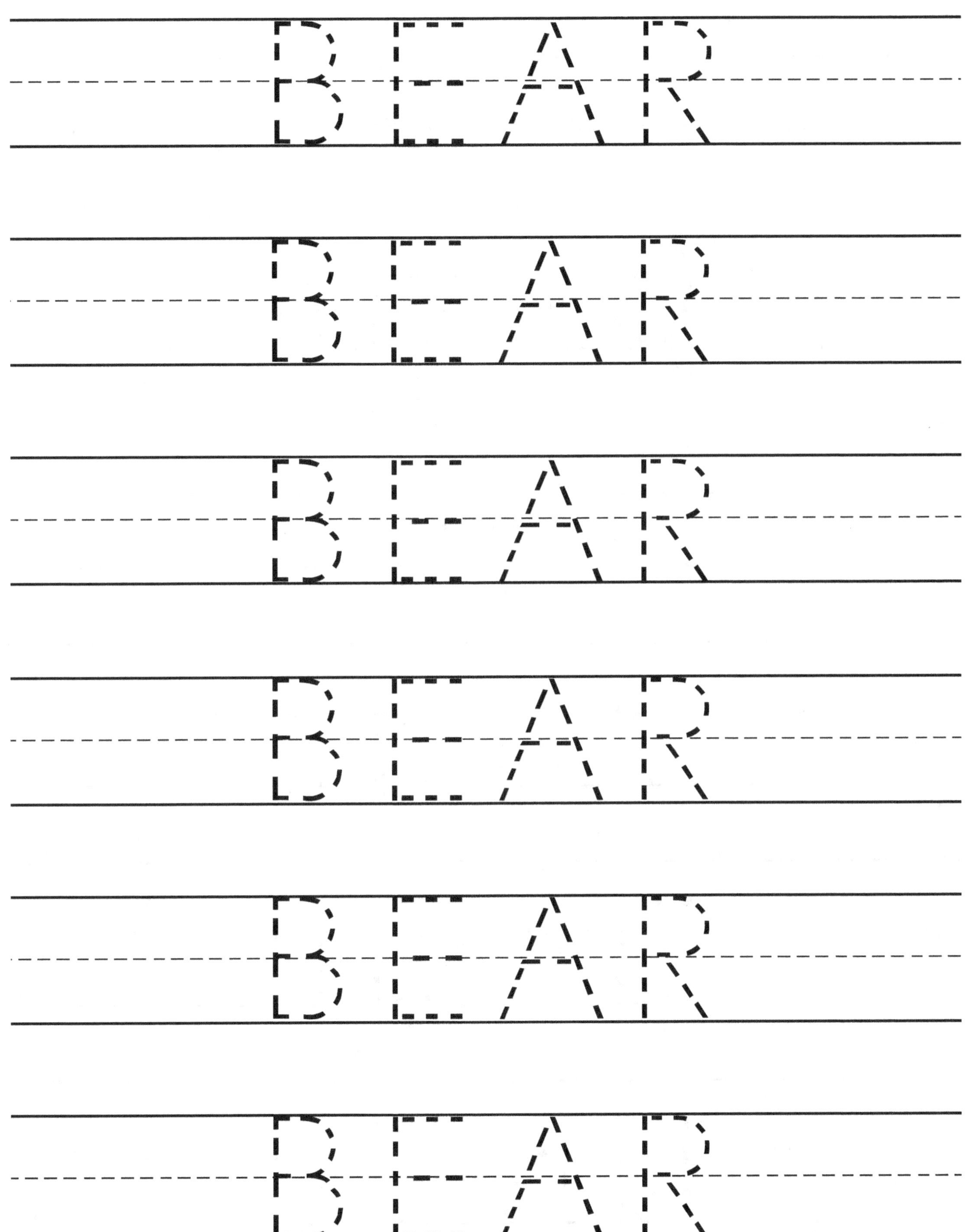

bear
bear
bear
bear
bear
bear

C is for

cat

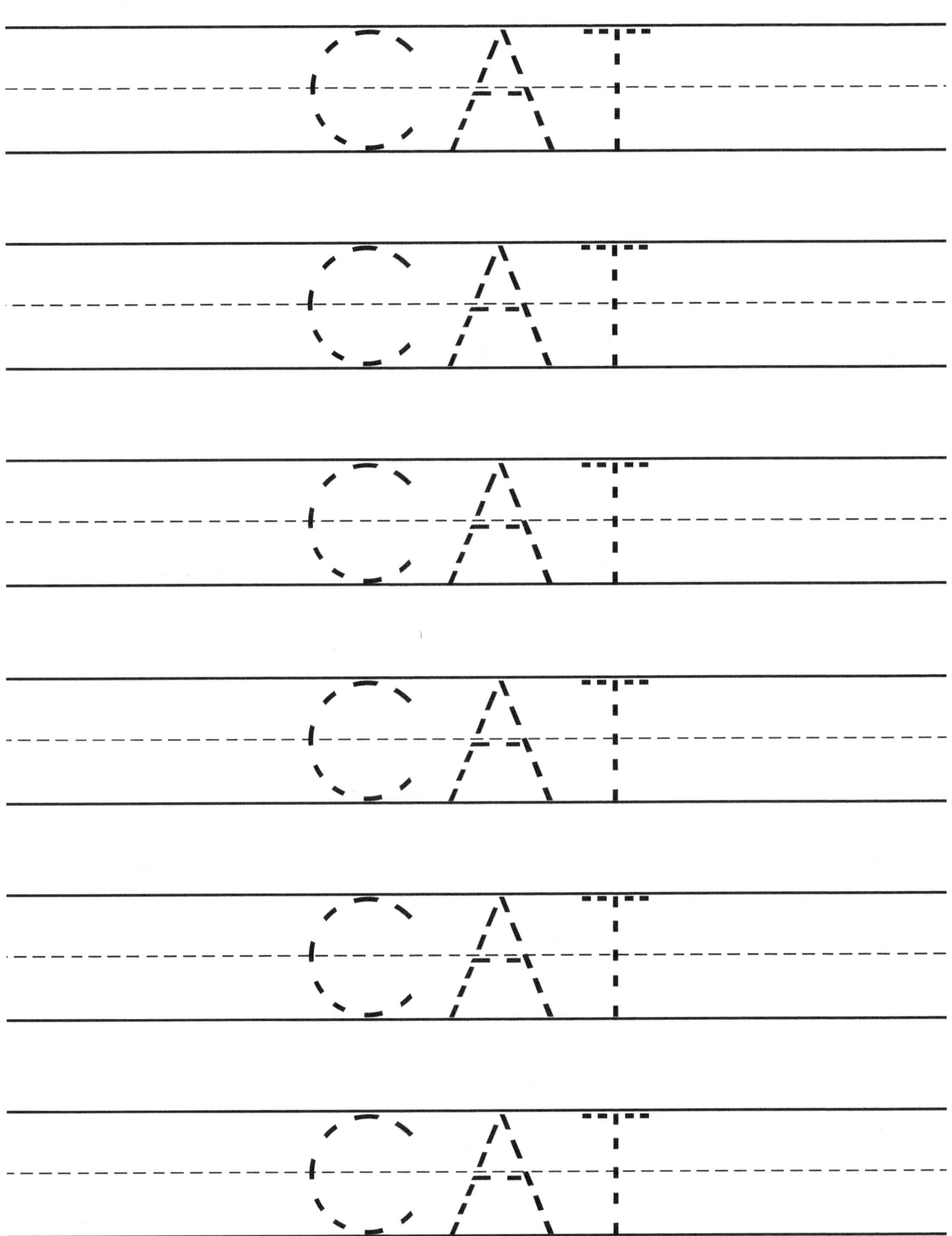

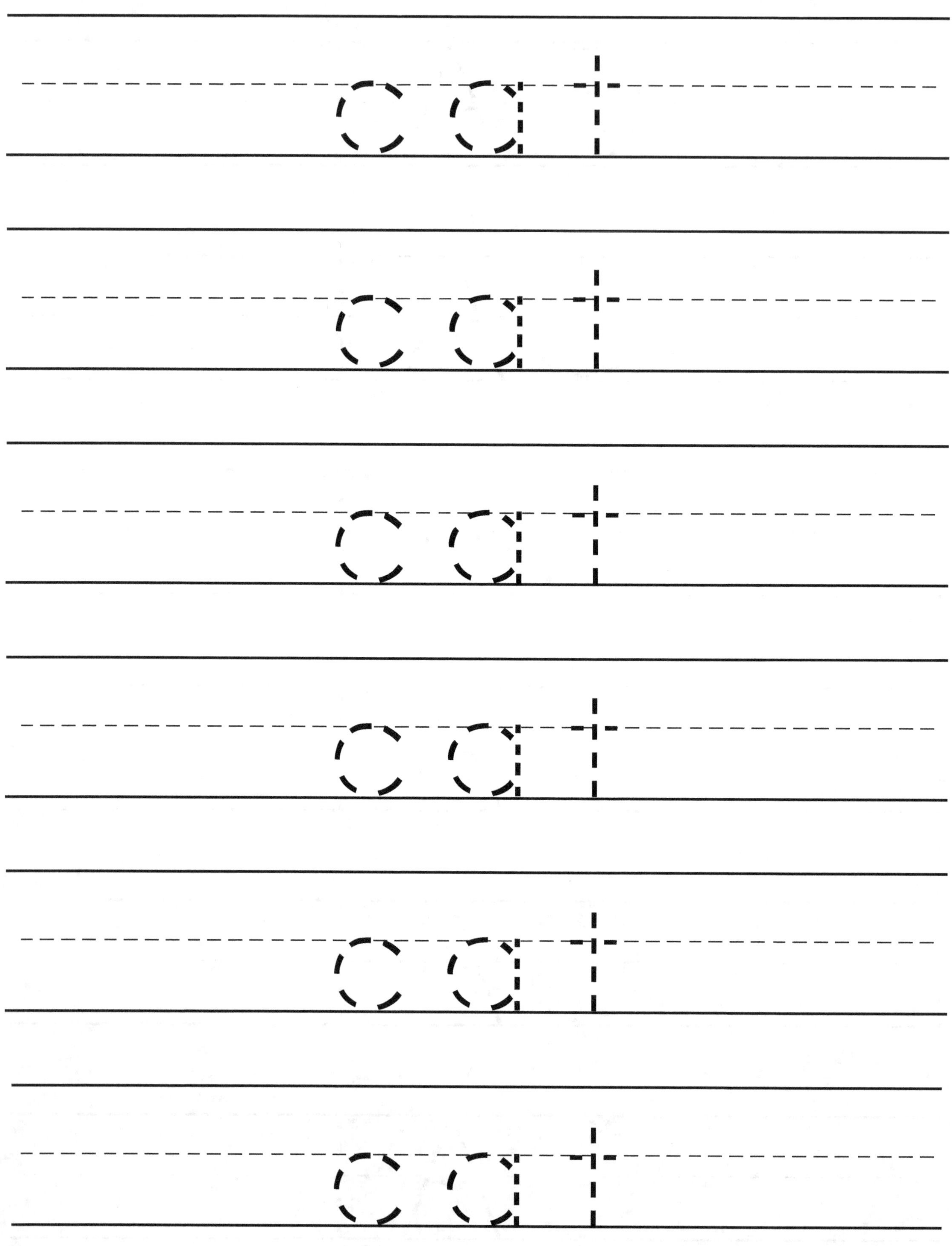
cat
cat
cat
cat
cat
cat

D is for

dolphin

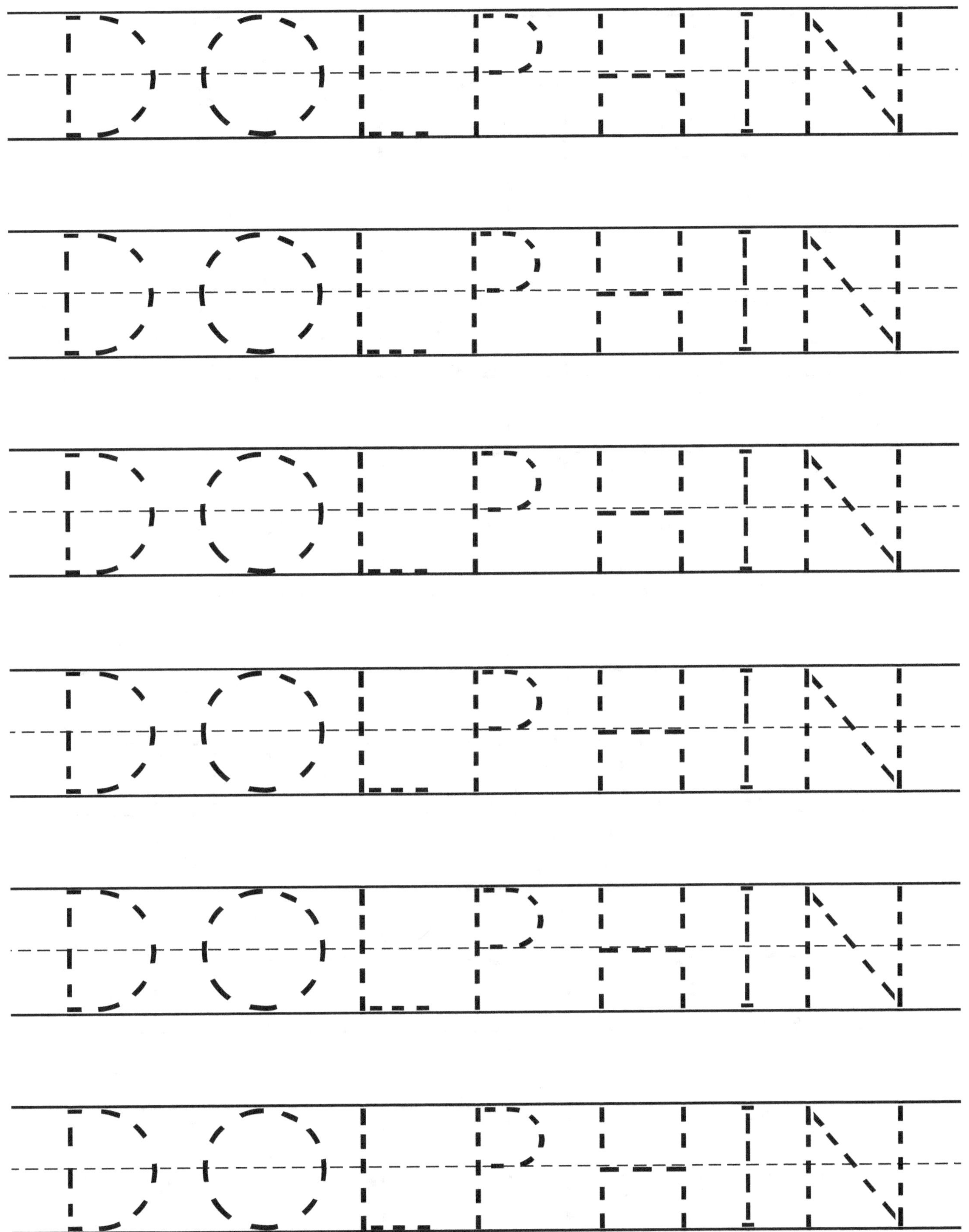

dolphin

dolphin

dolphin

dolphin

dolphin

dolphin

E is for

elephant

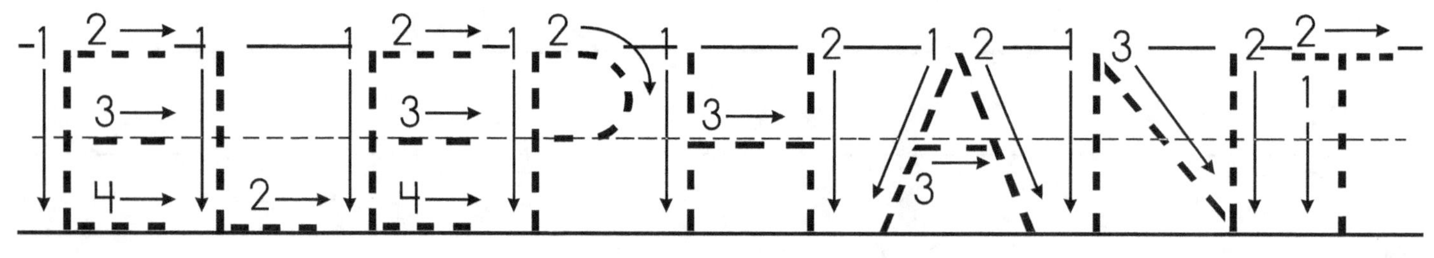

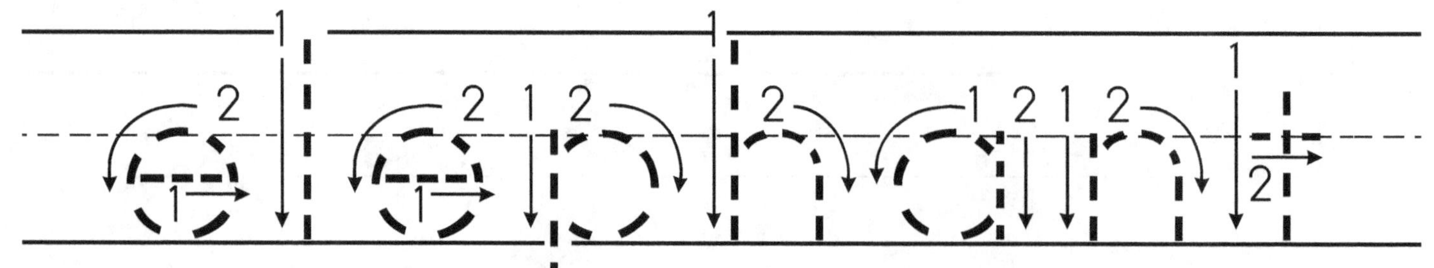

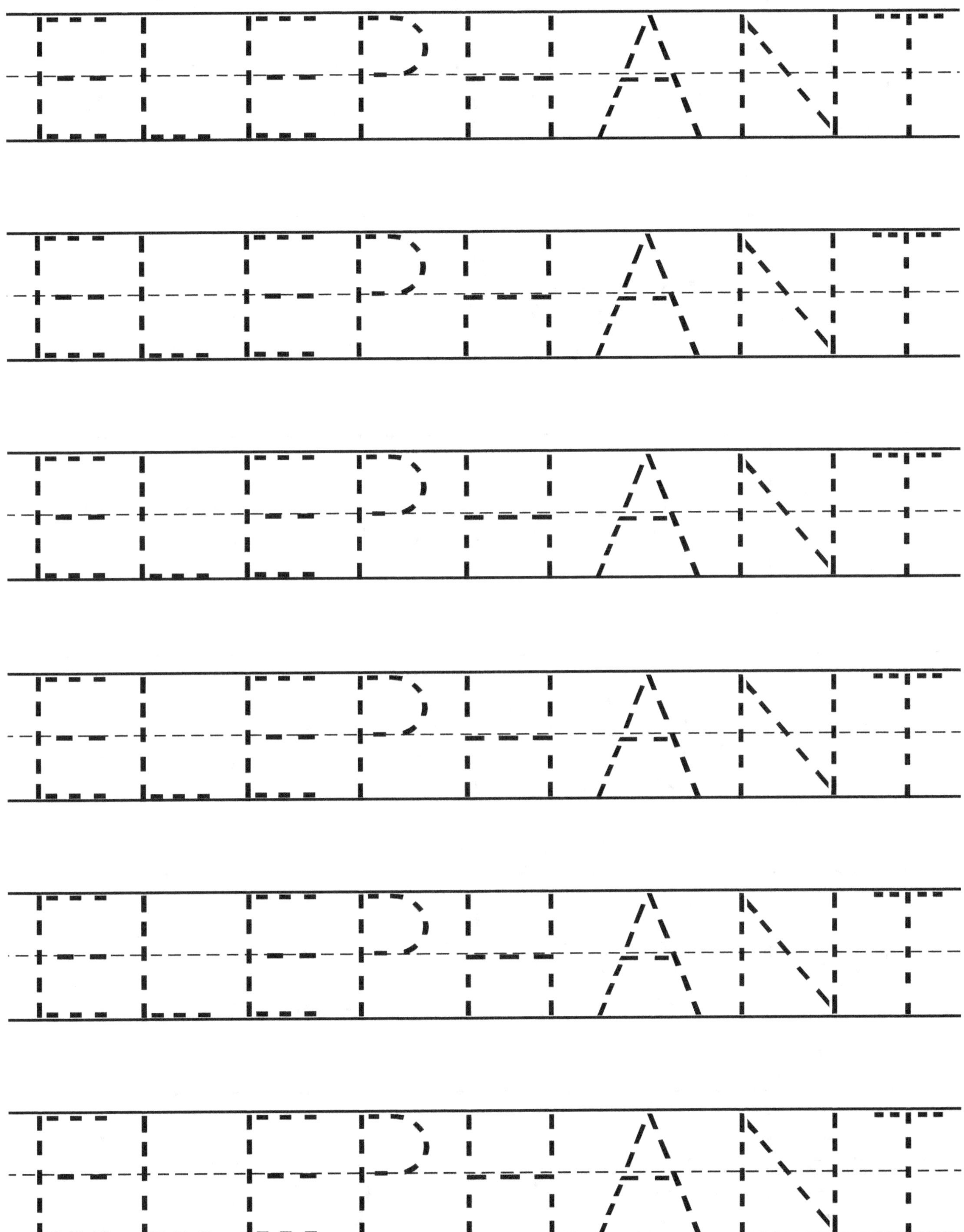

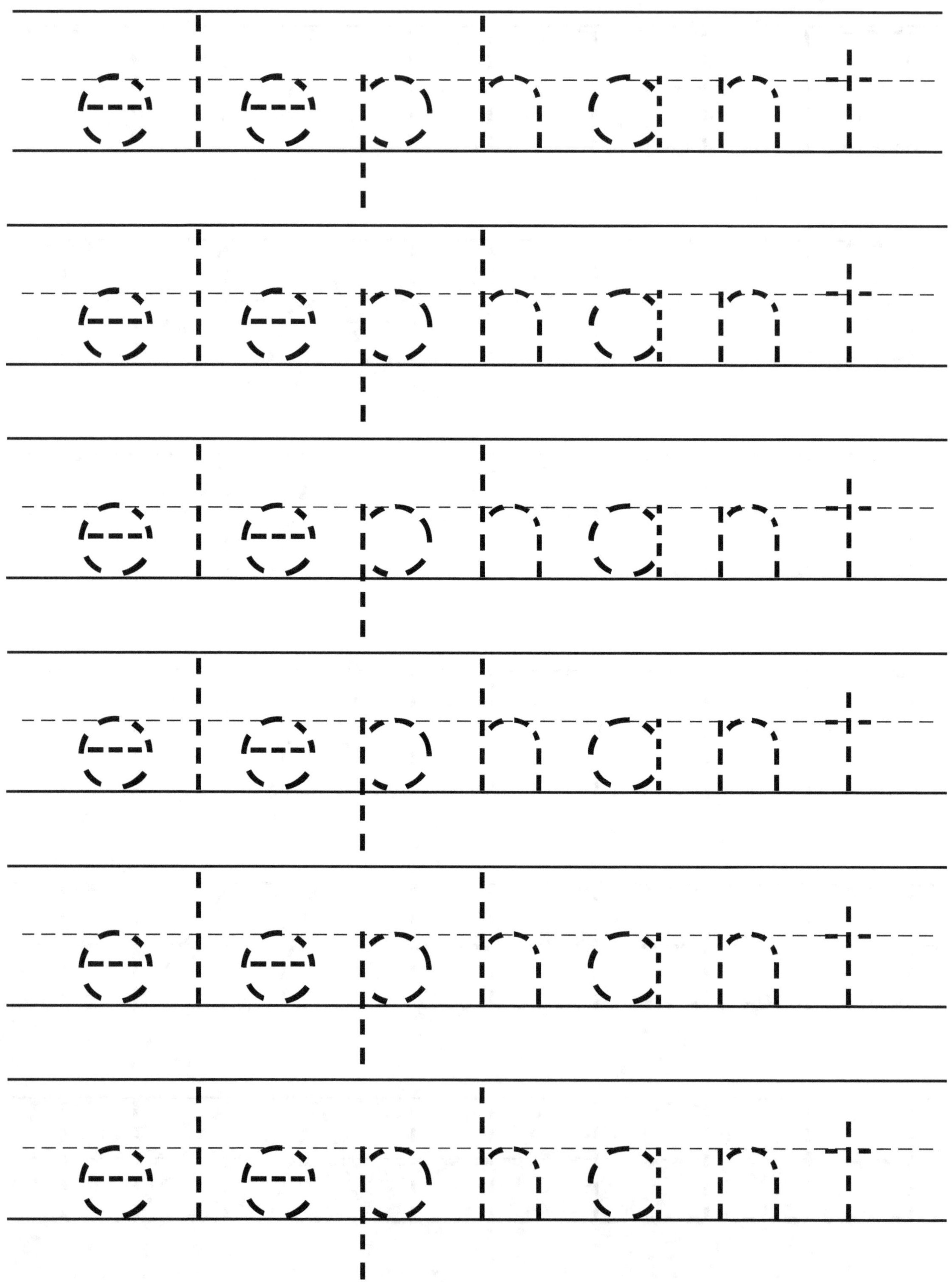
elephant
elephant
elephant
elephant
elephant
elephant

F is for

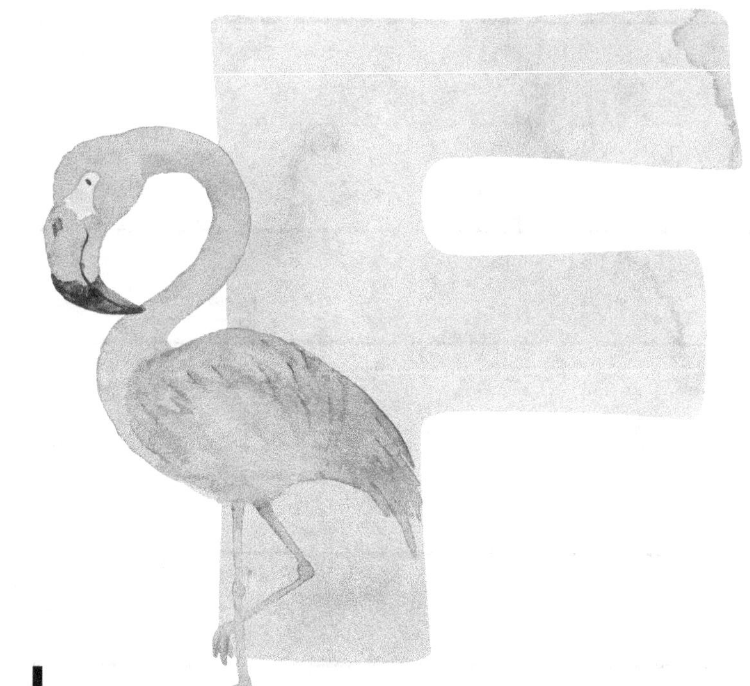

flamingo

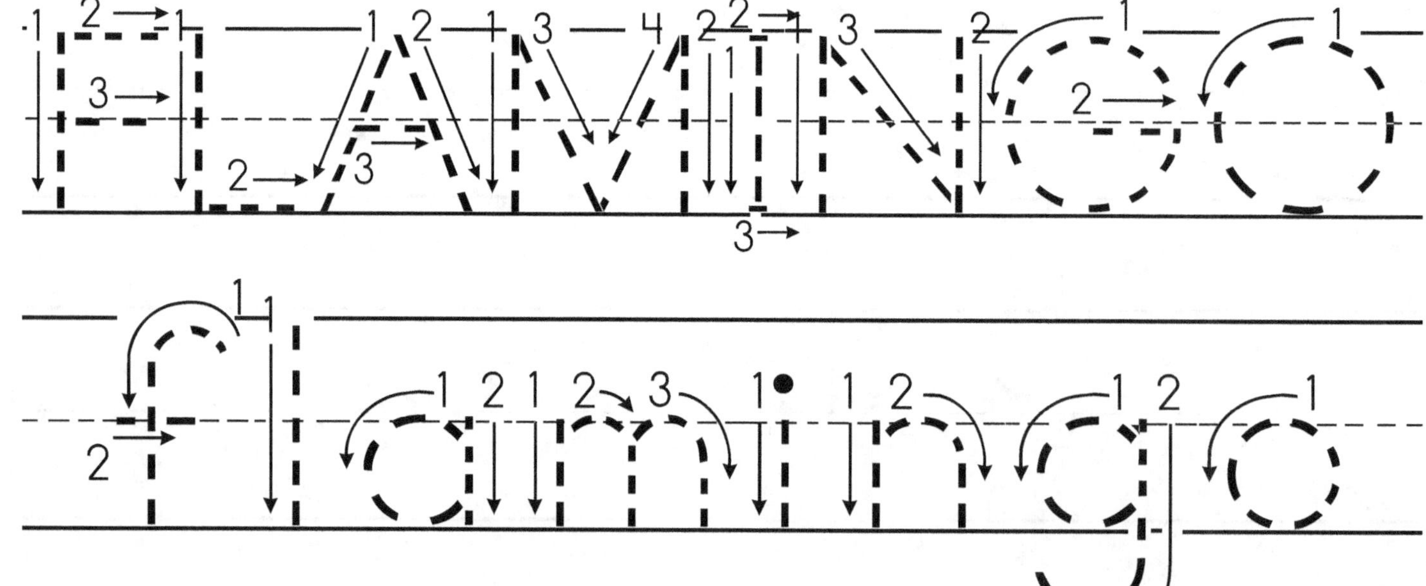

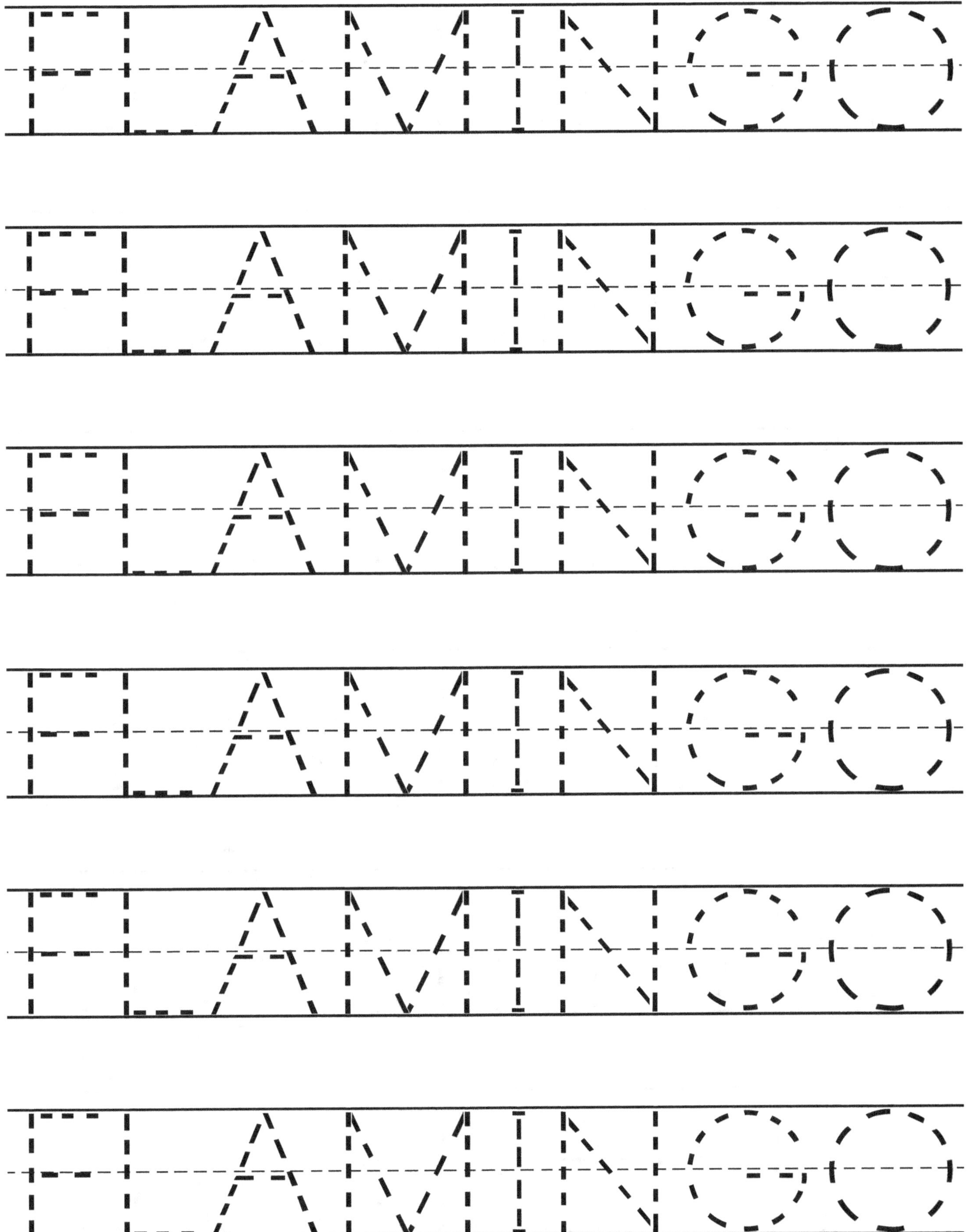

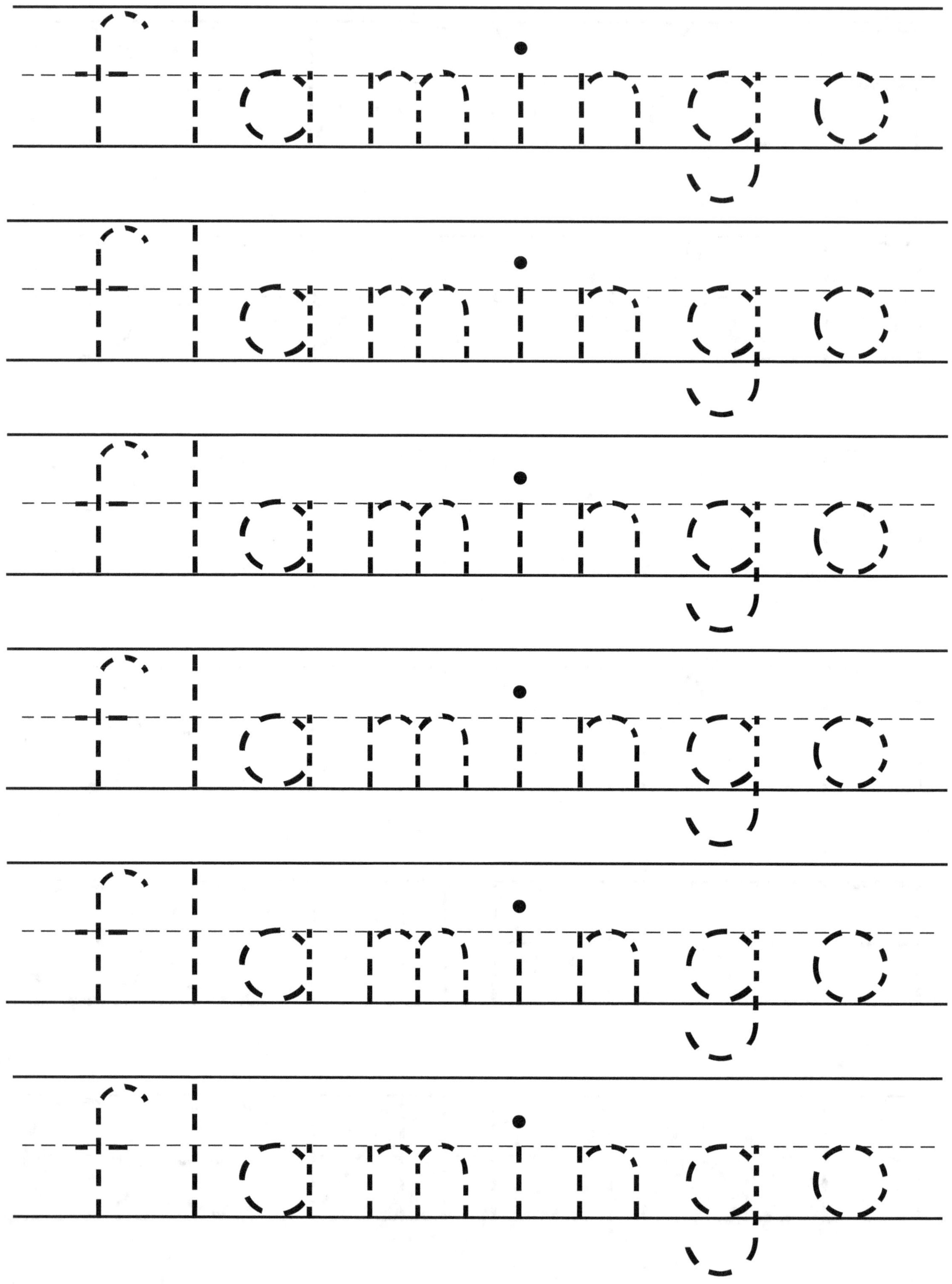flamingo
flamingo
flamingo
flamingo
flamingo
flamingo

G is for

giraffe

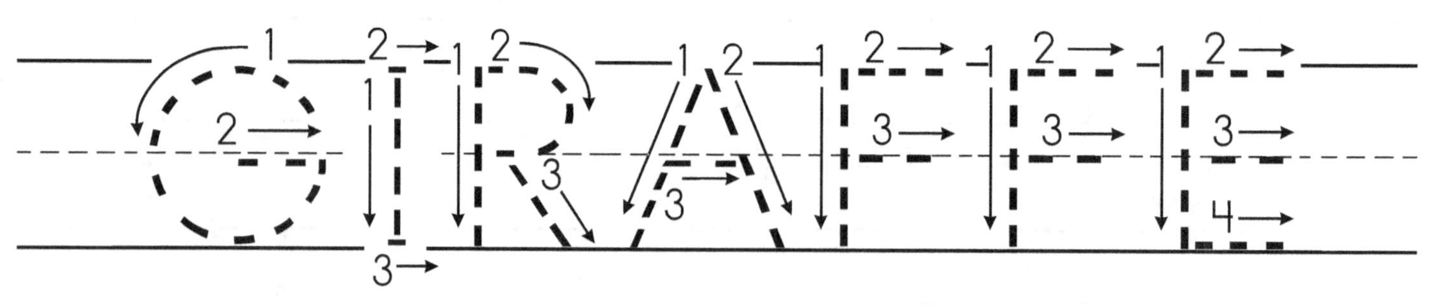

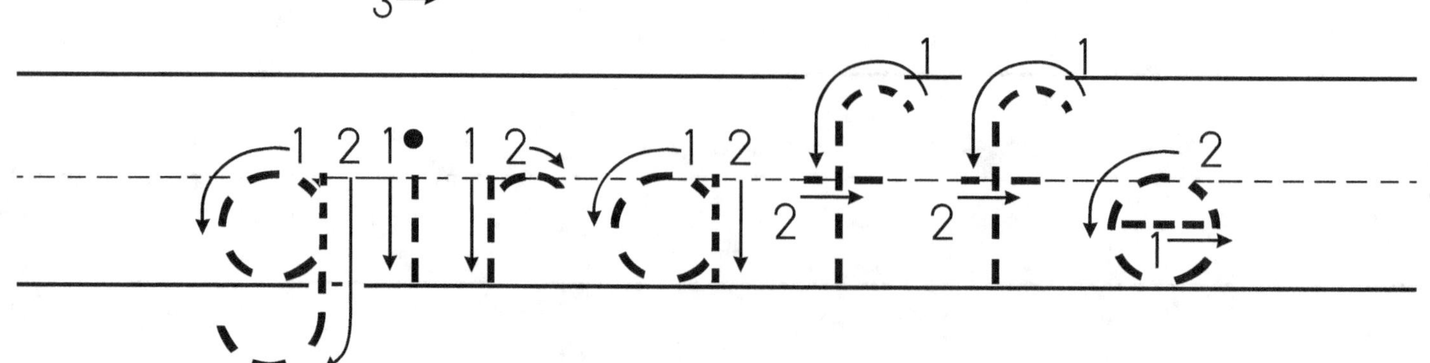

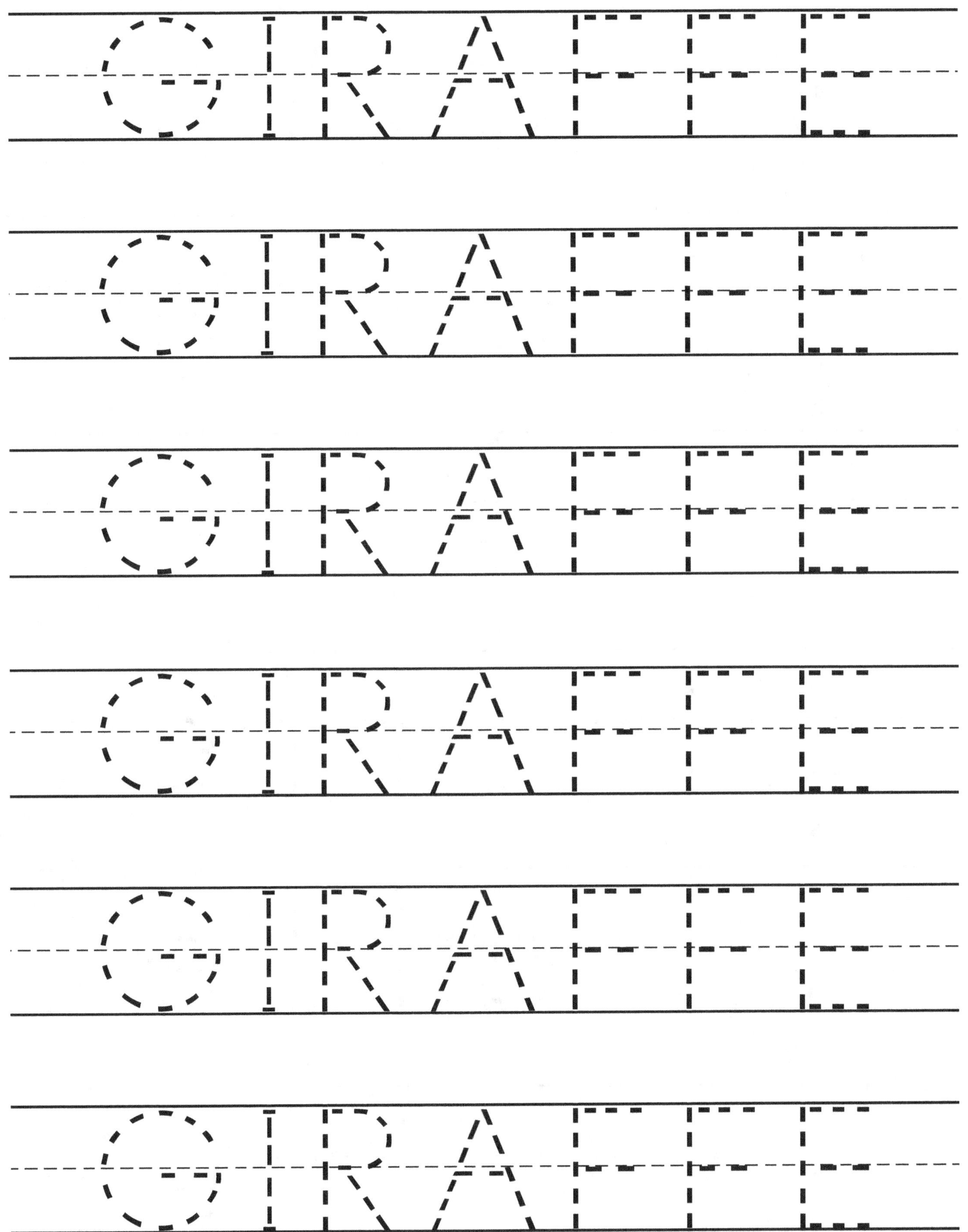

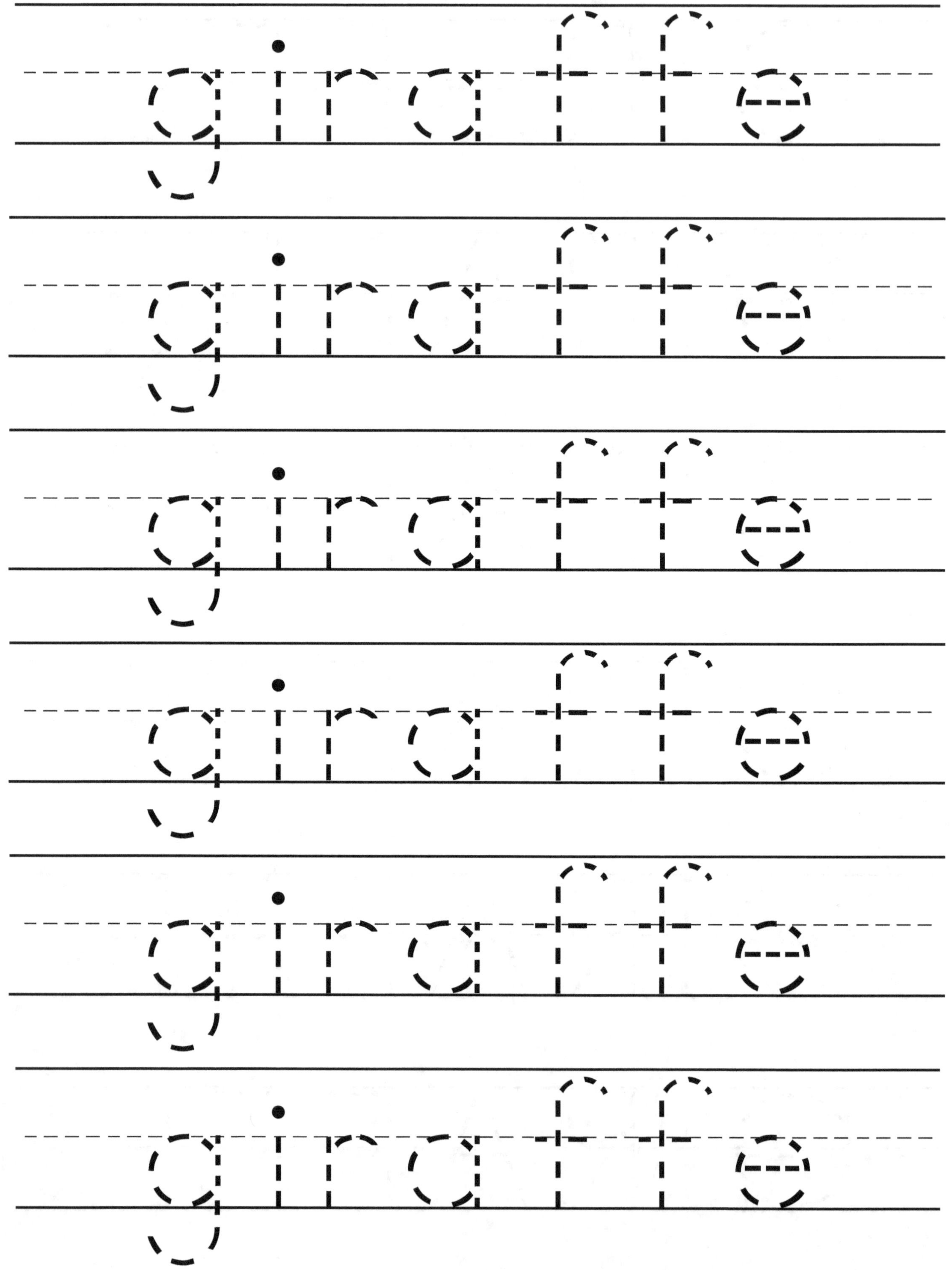

H is for

hippo

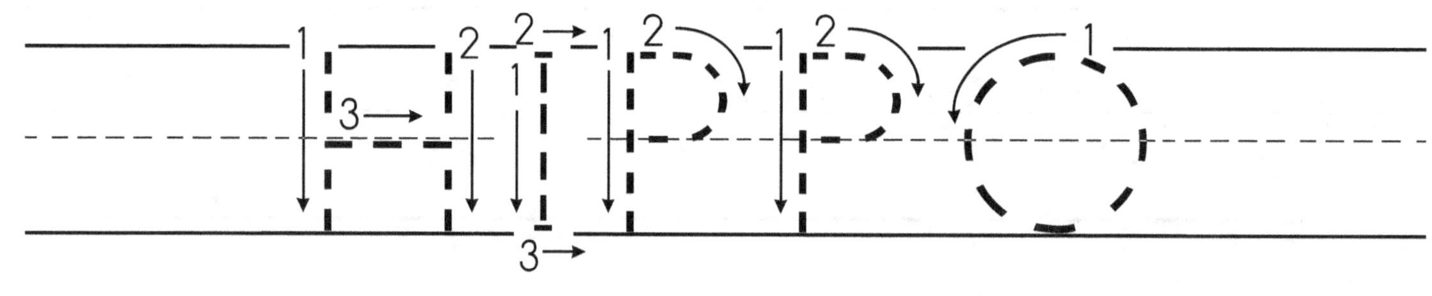

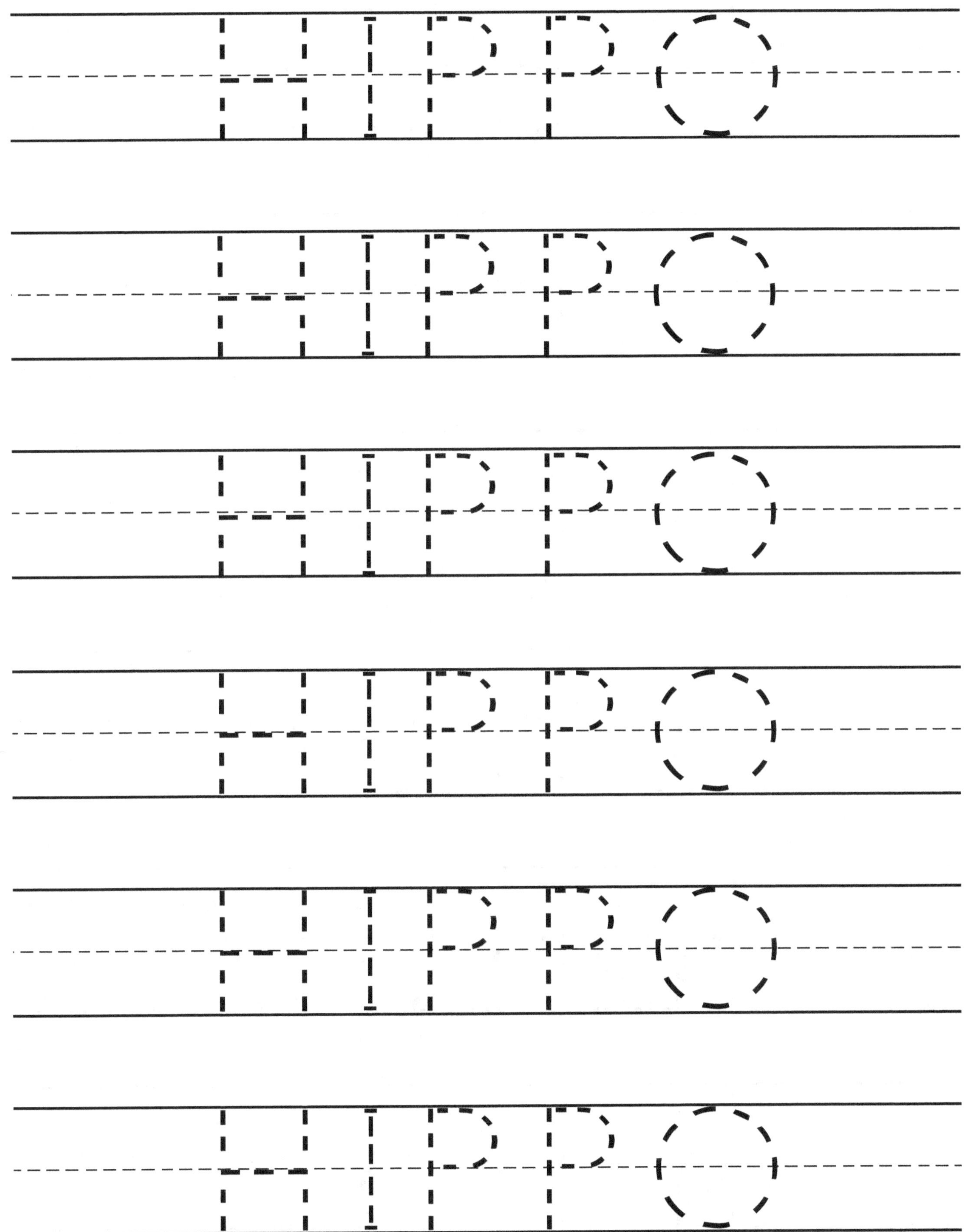

hippo

hippo

hippo

hippo

hippo

hippo

I is for

iguana

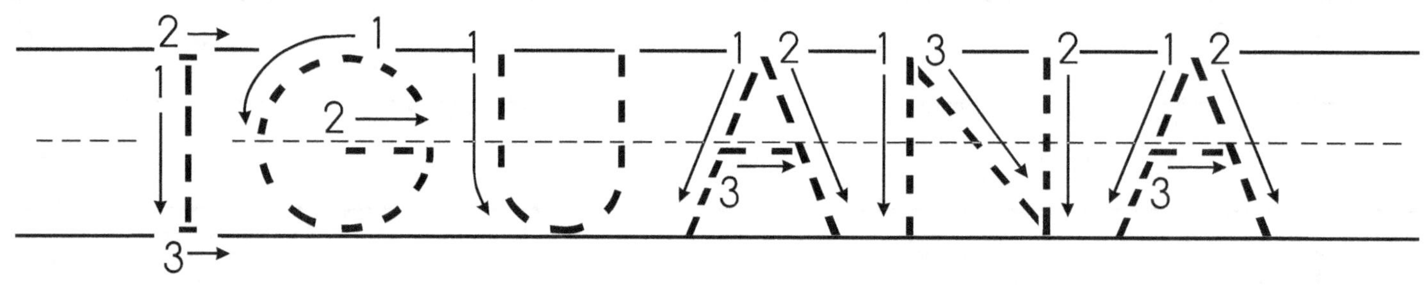

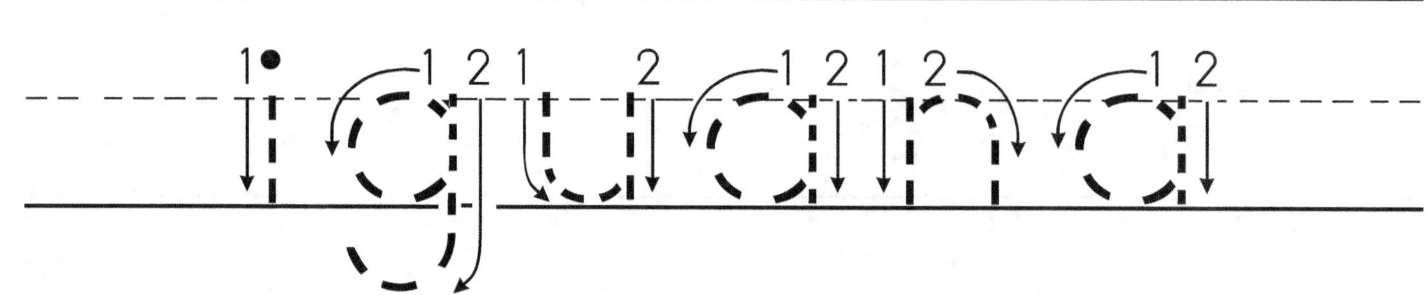

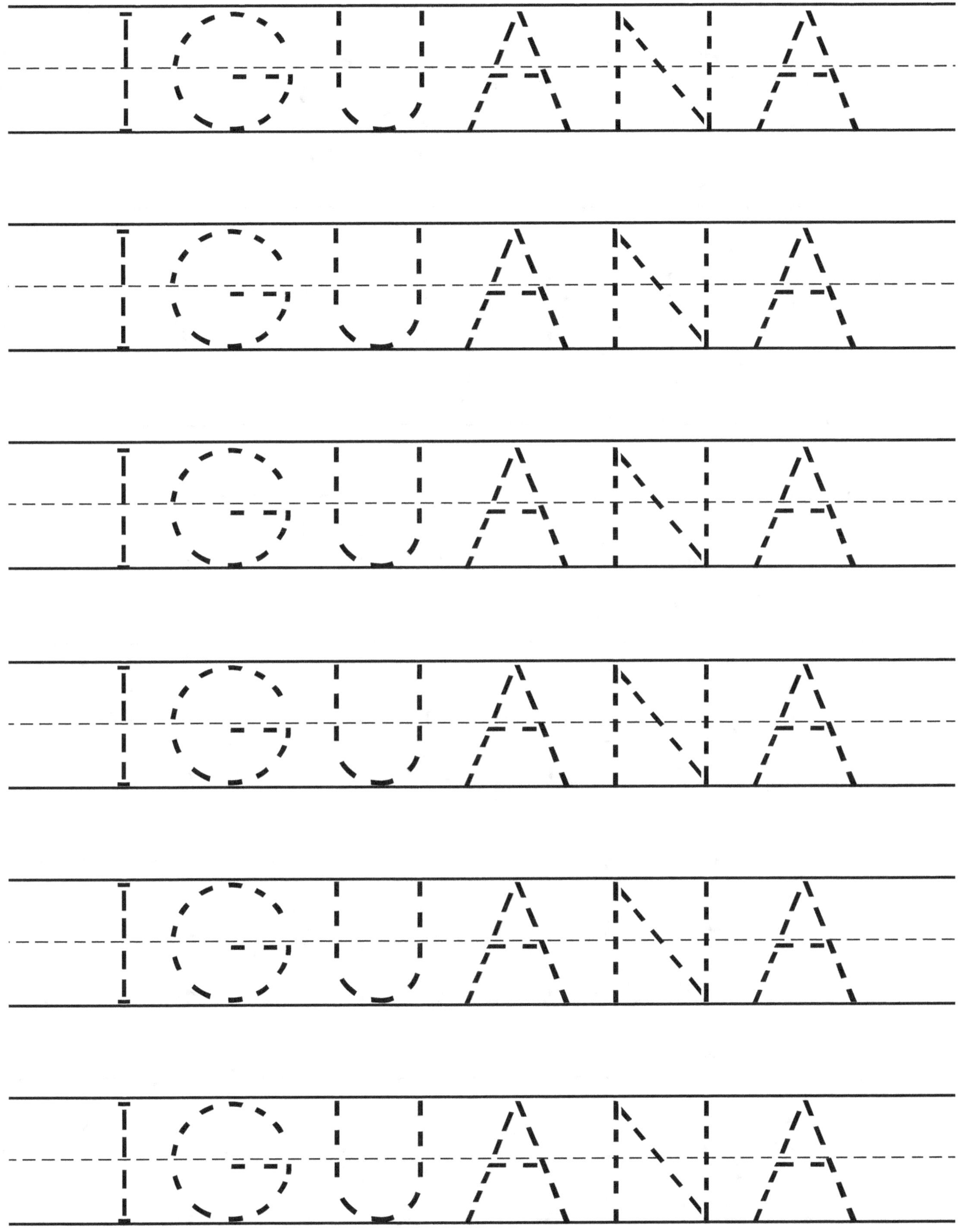

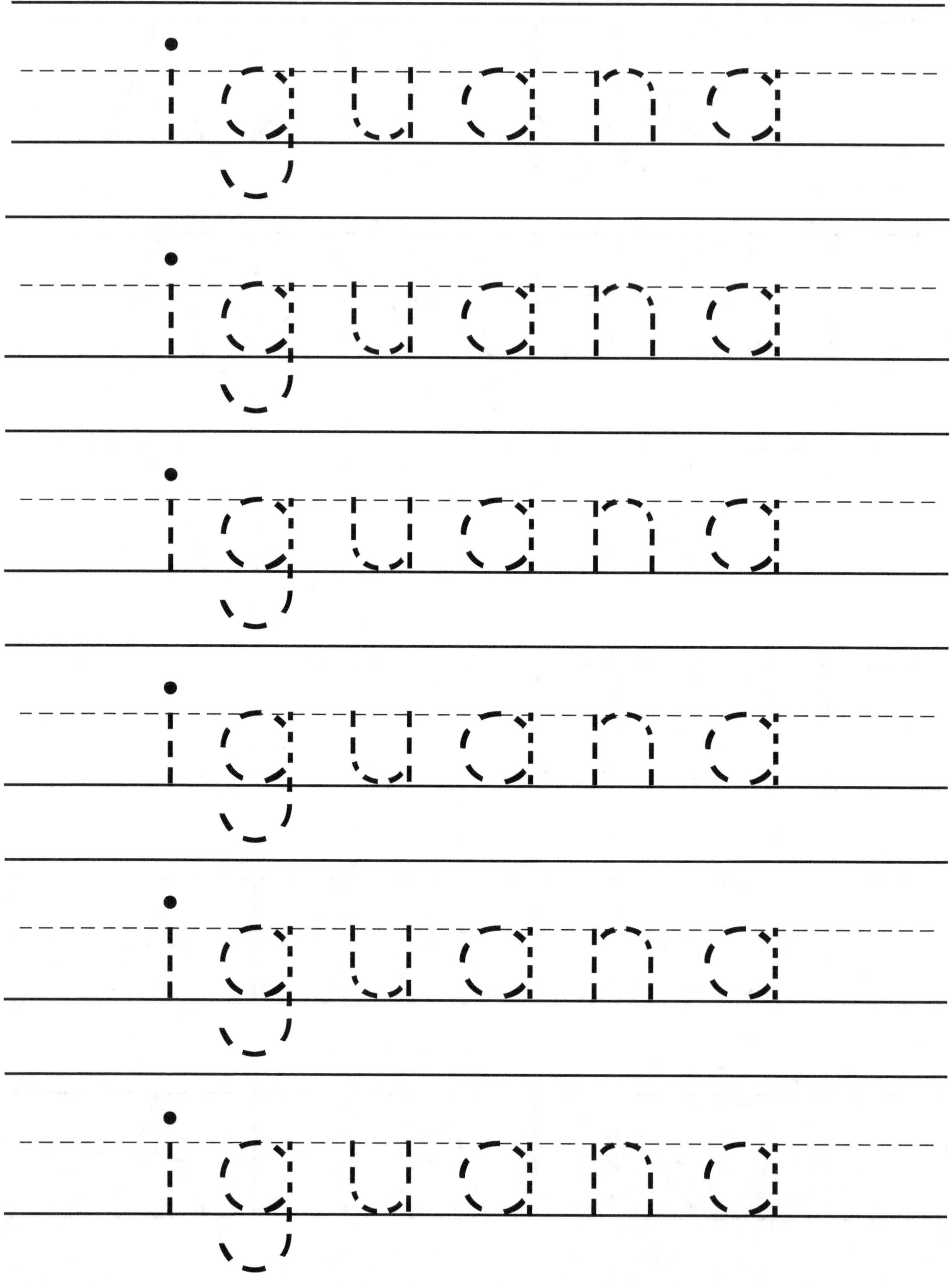

iguana
iguana
iguana
iguana
iguana
iguana

J is for

jellyfish

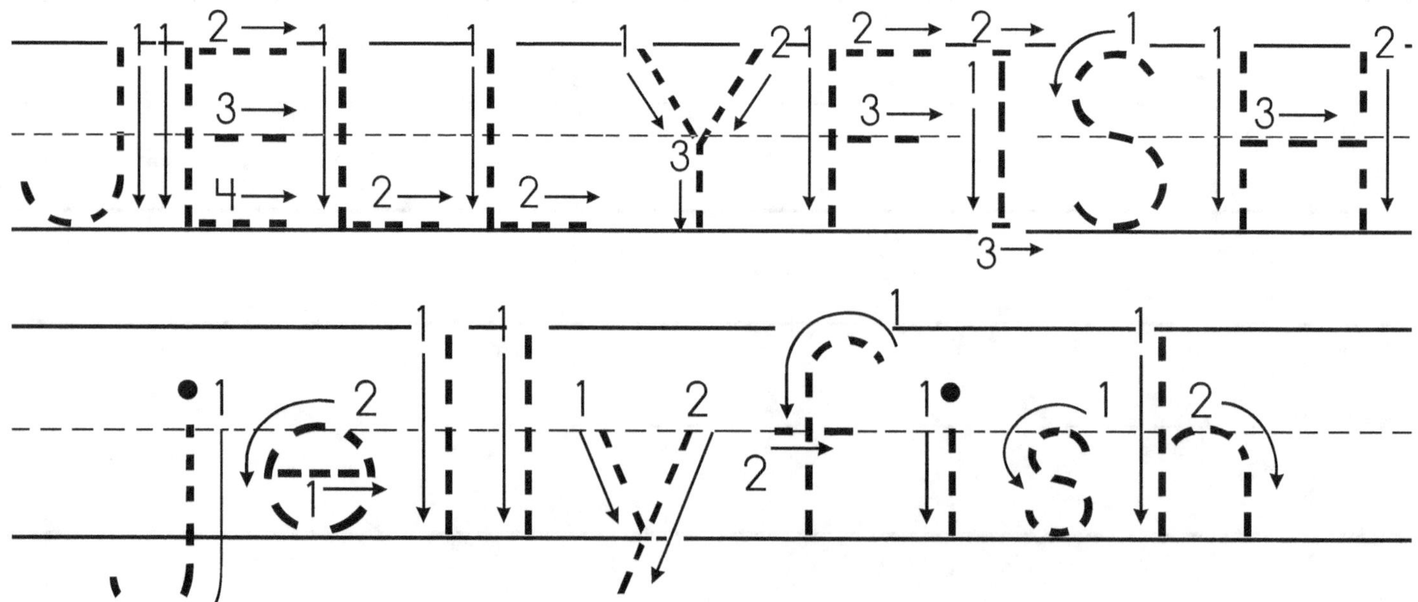

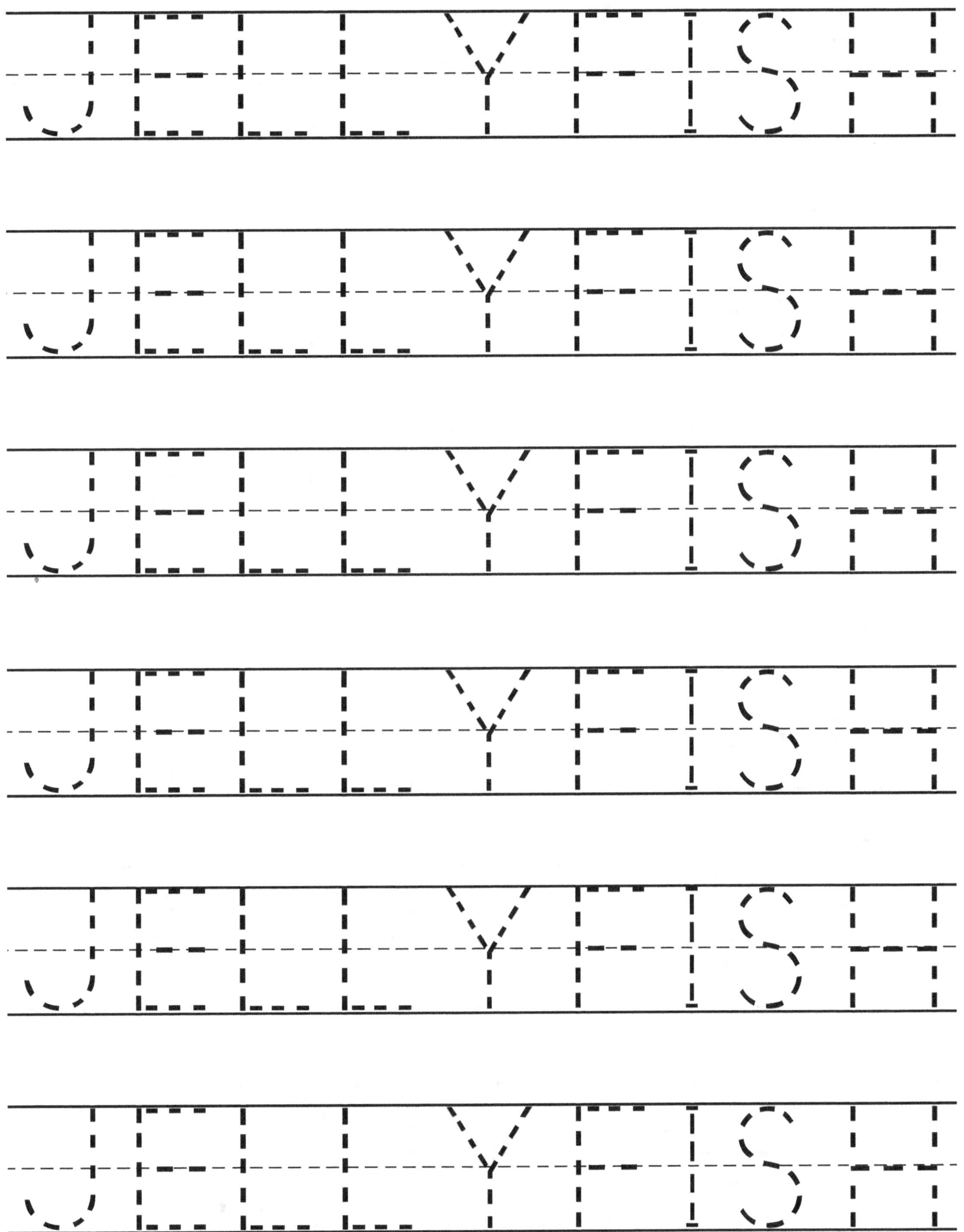

JELLYFISH
JELLYFISH
JELLYFISH
JELLYFISH
JELLYFISH
JELLYFISH

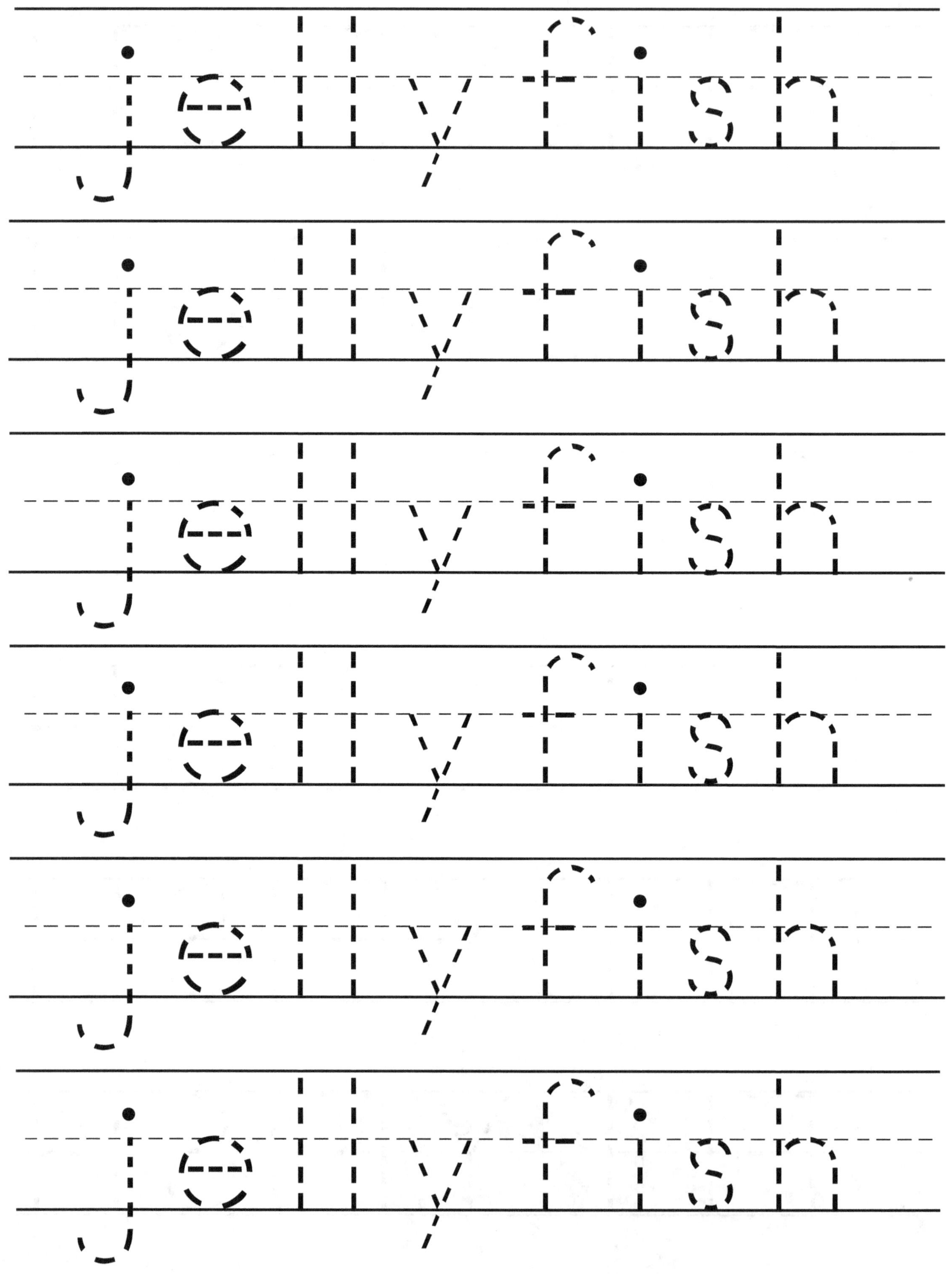

K is for

kangaroo

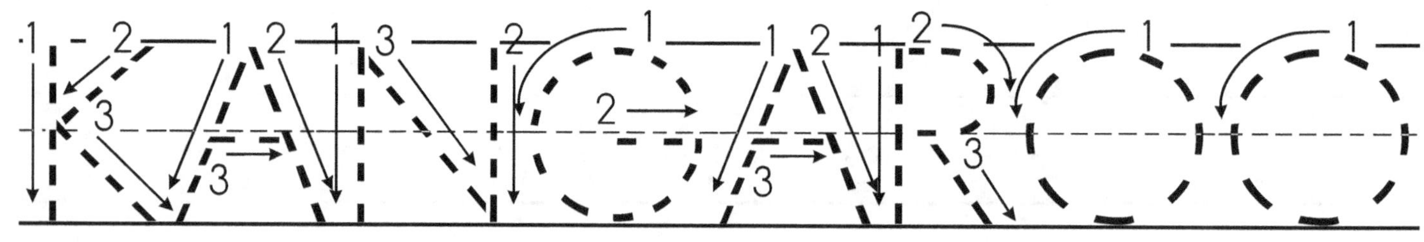

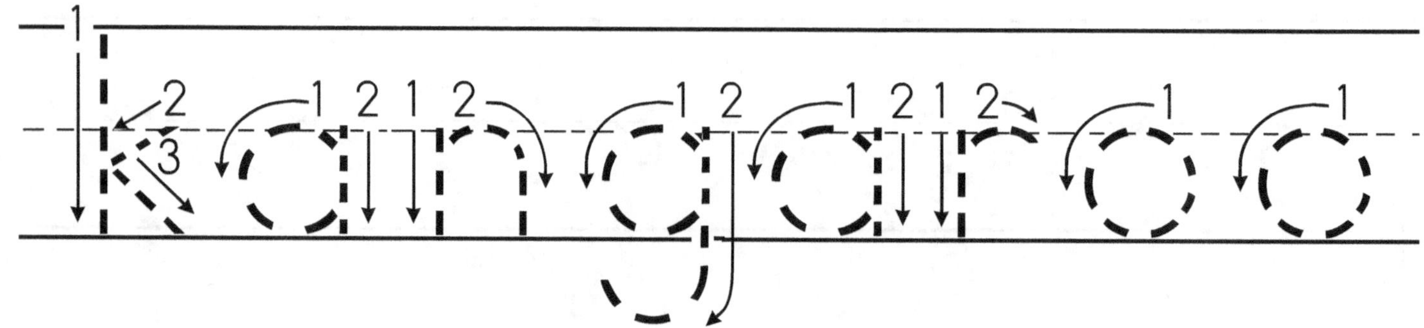

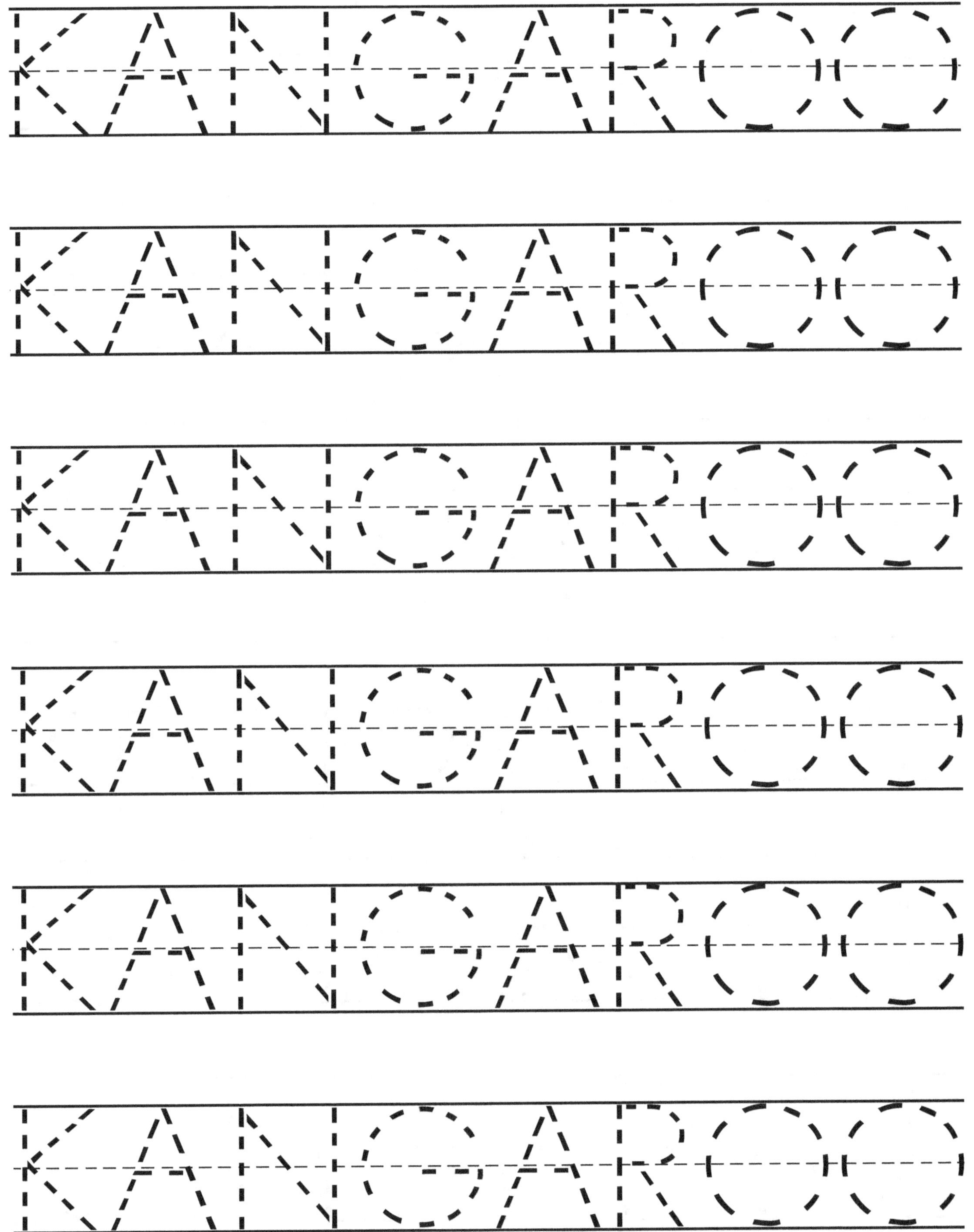

kangaroo

kangaroo

kangaroo

kangaroo

kangaroo

kangaroo

L is for

lion

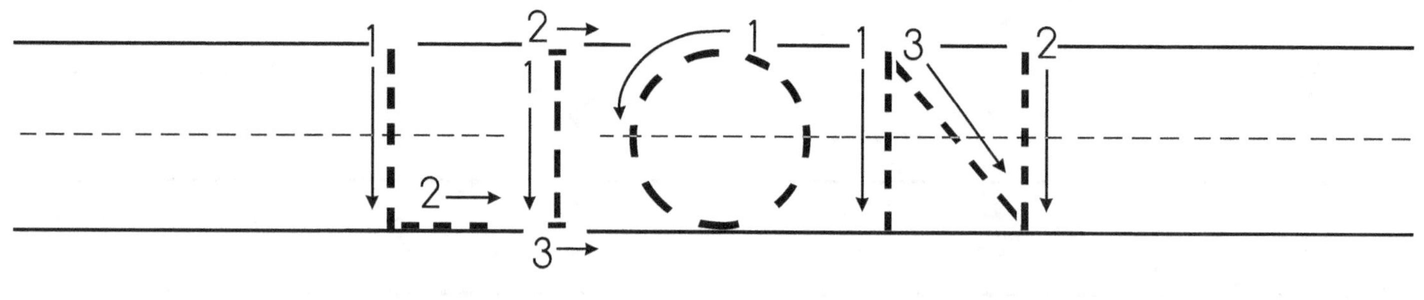

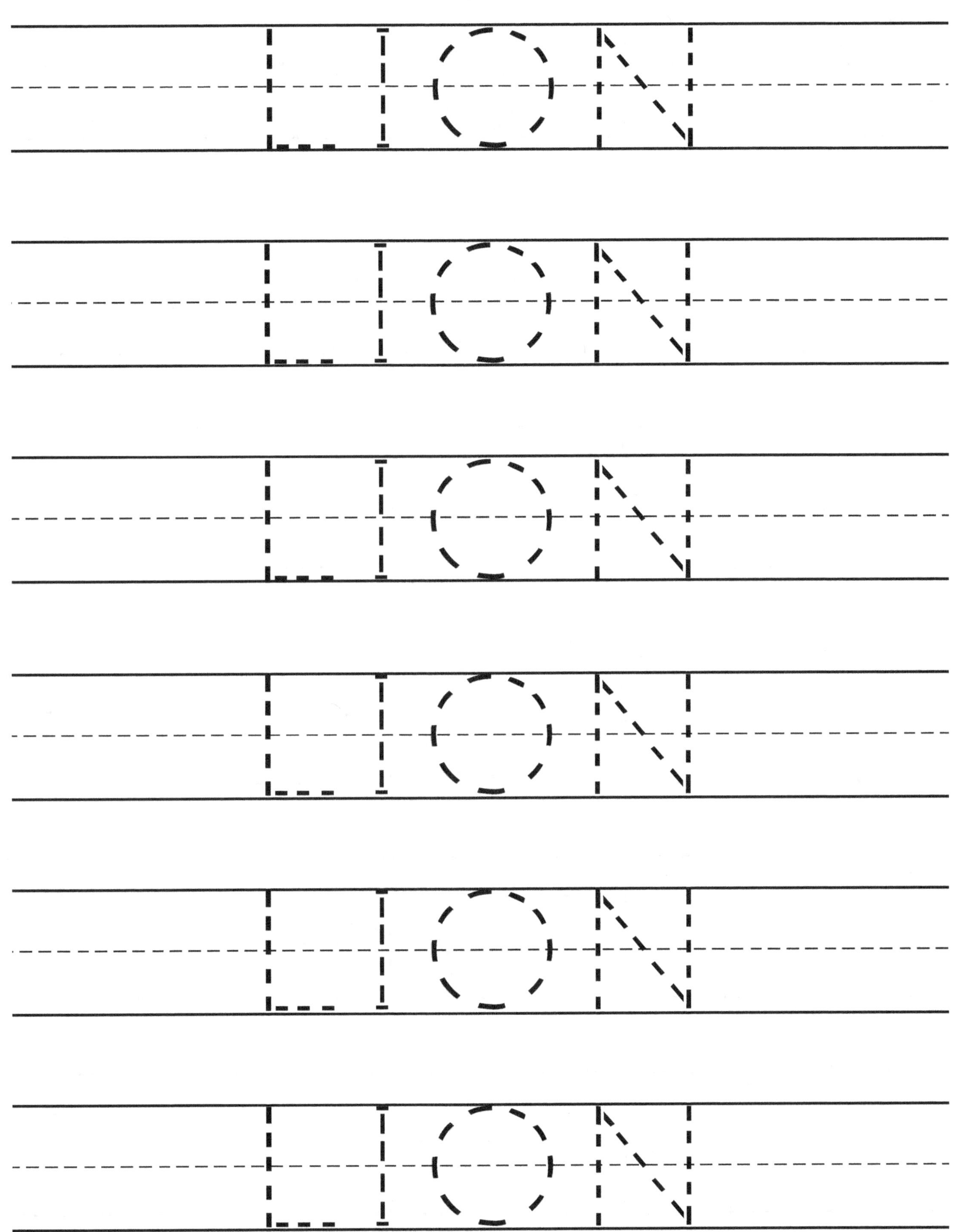

lion

lion

lion

lion

lion

lion

M is for

monkey

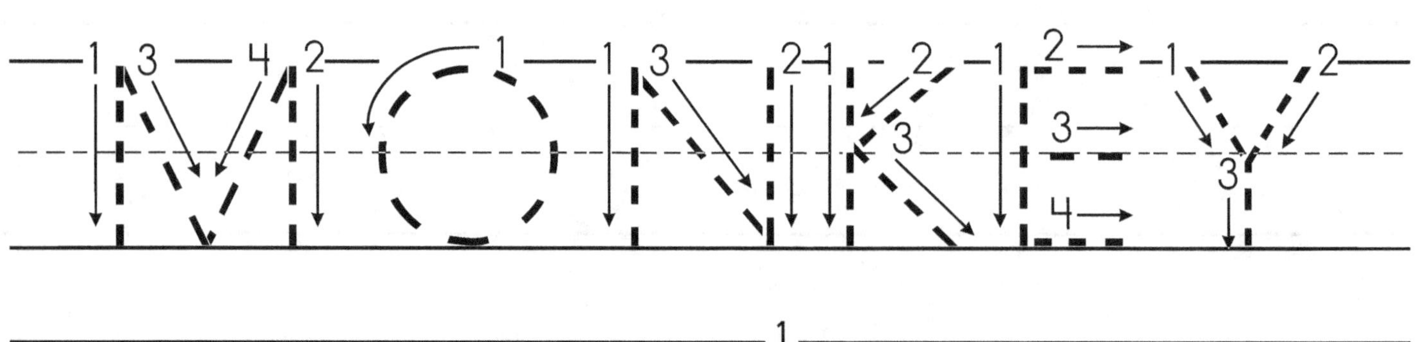

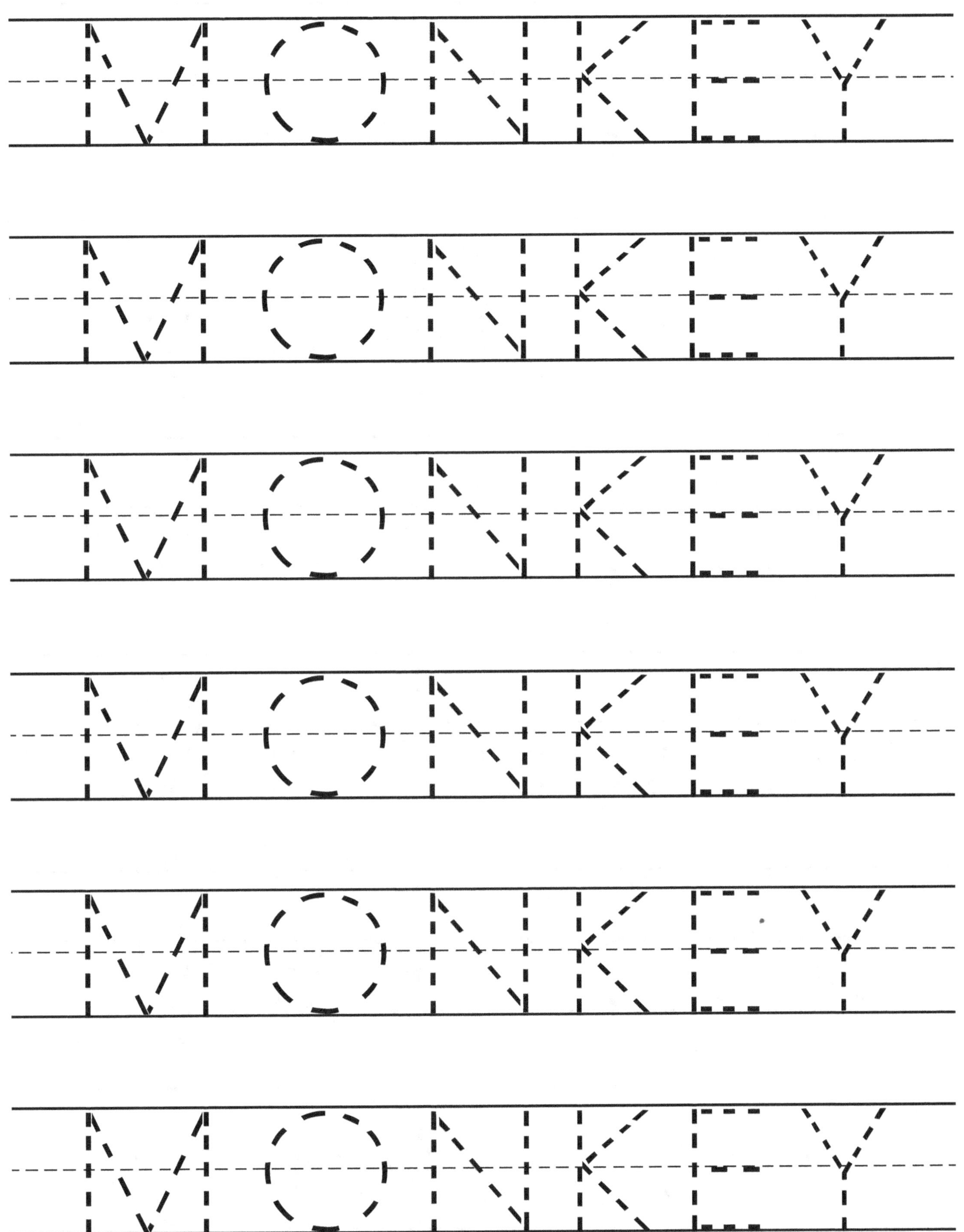

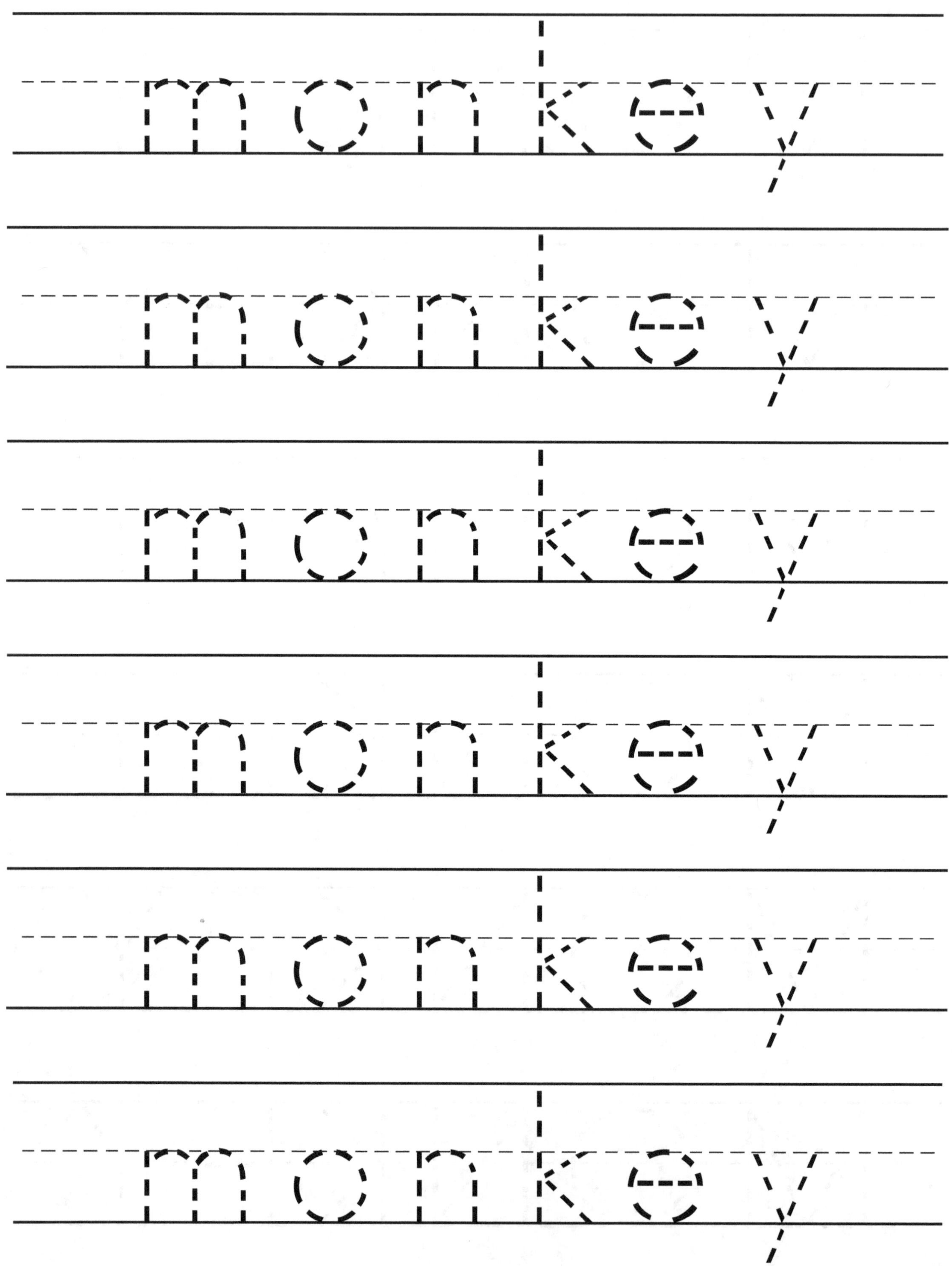
monkey
monkey
monkey
monkey
monkey
monkey

N is for

newt

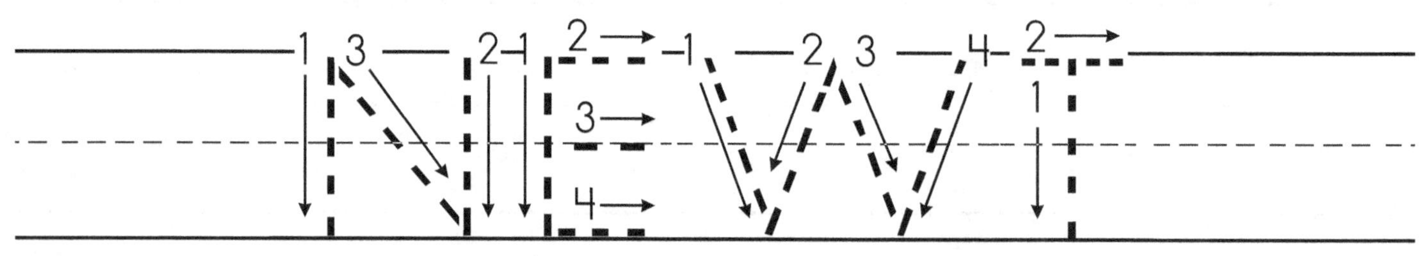

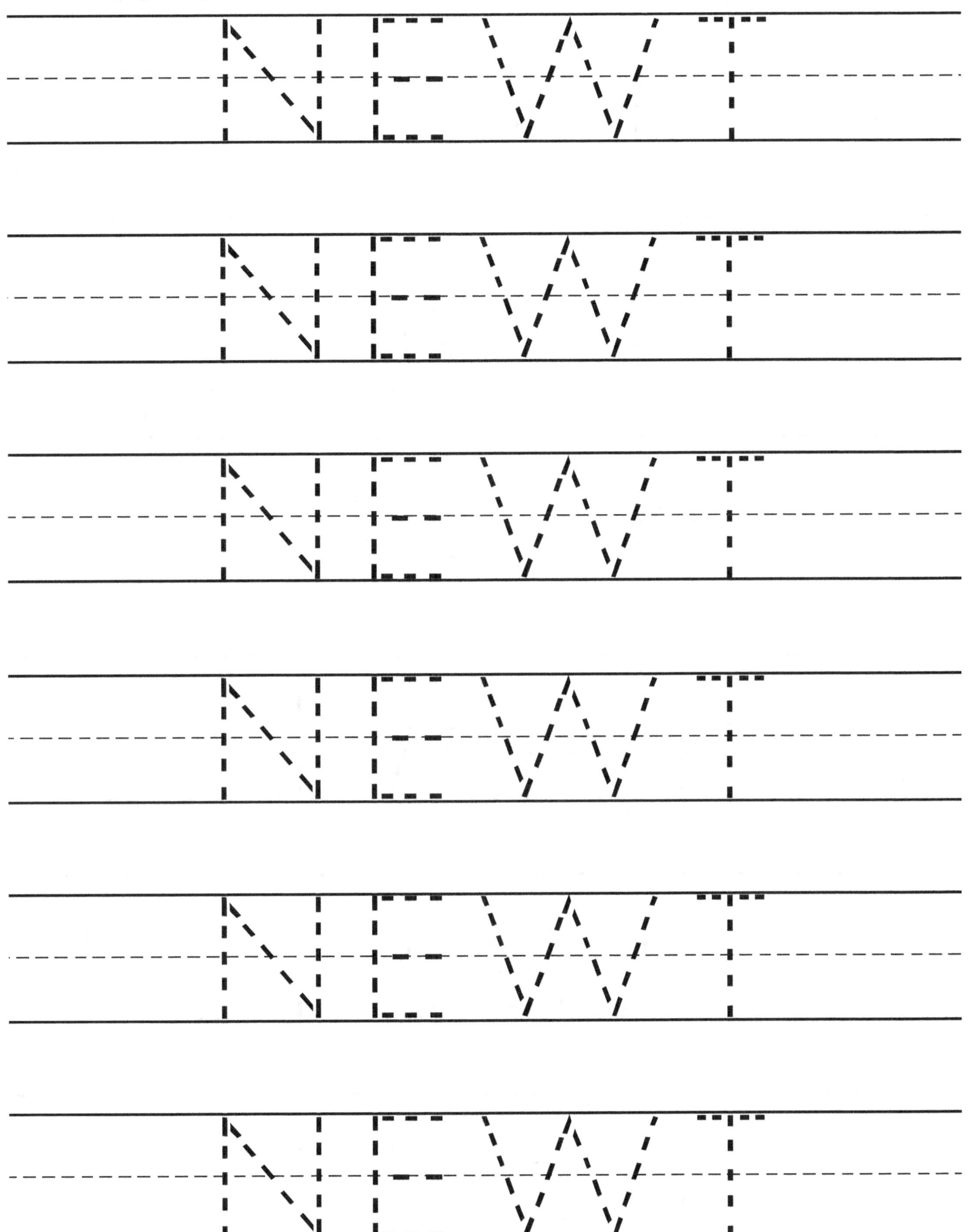

newt
newt
newt
newt
newt
newt

O is for

owl

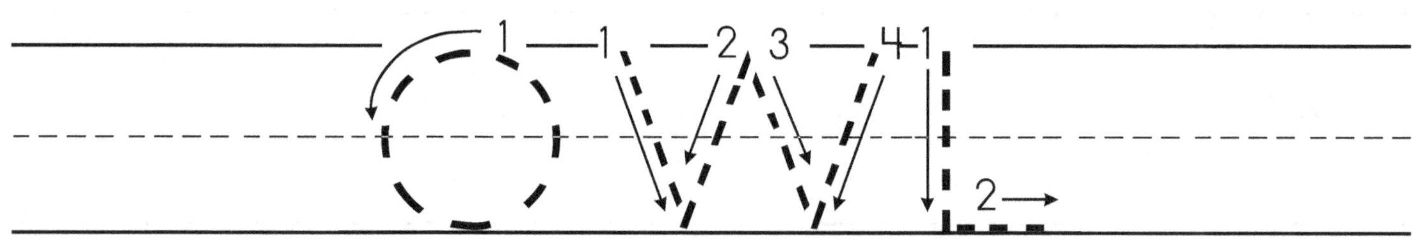

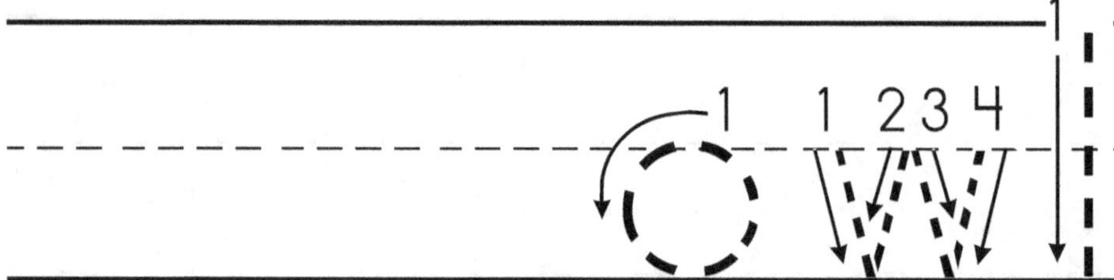

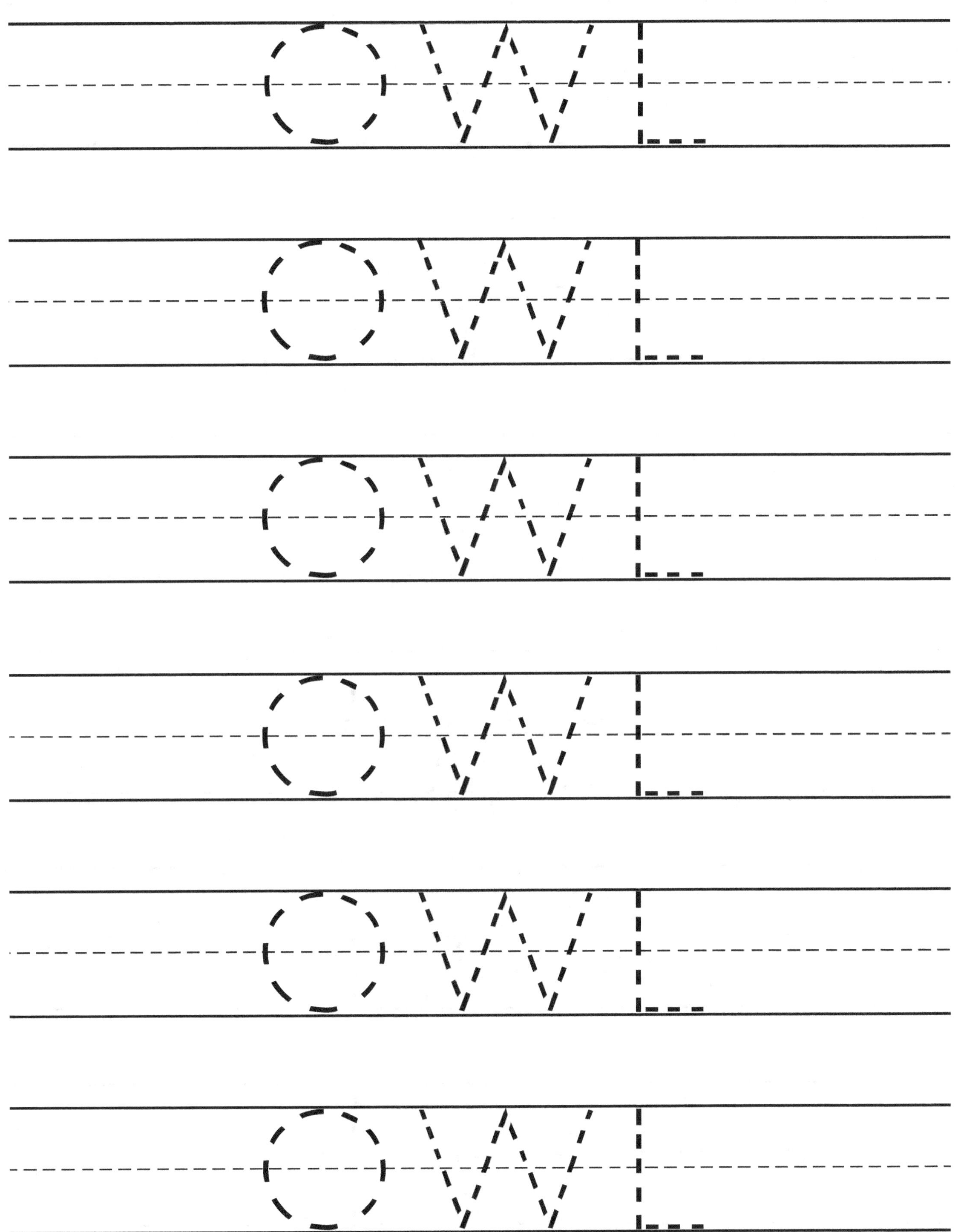

ow

ow

ow

ow

ow

ow

P is for

panda

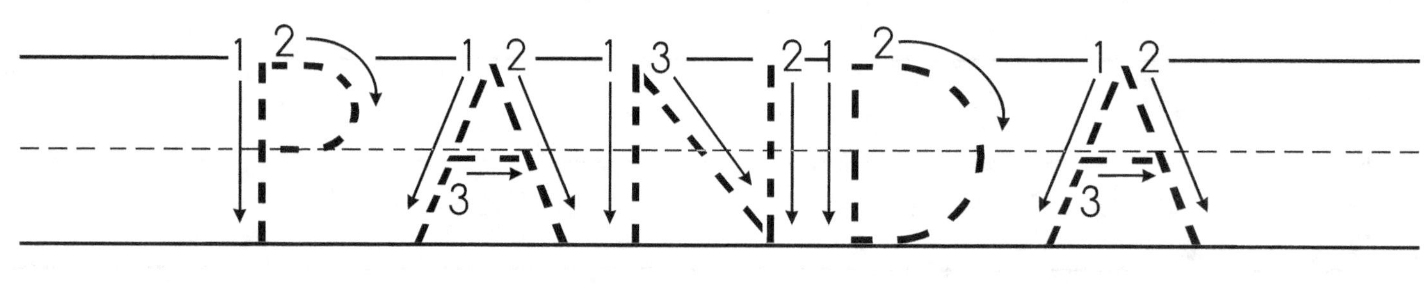

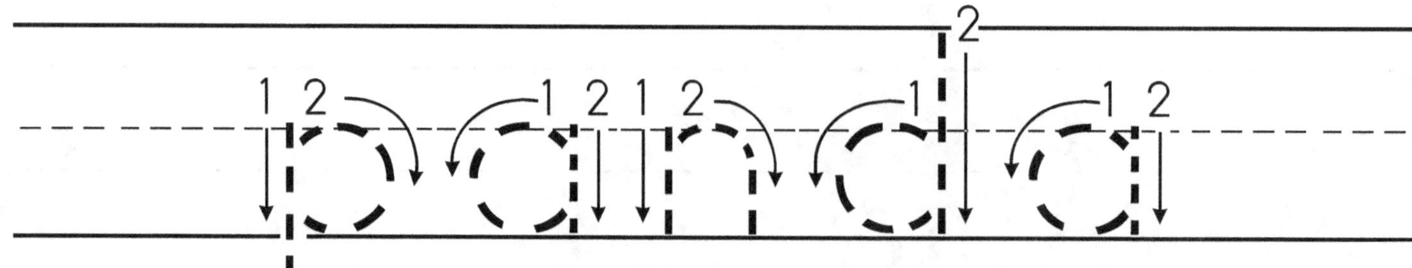

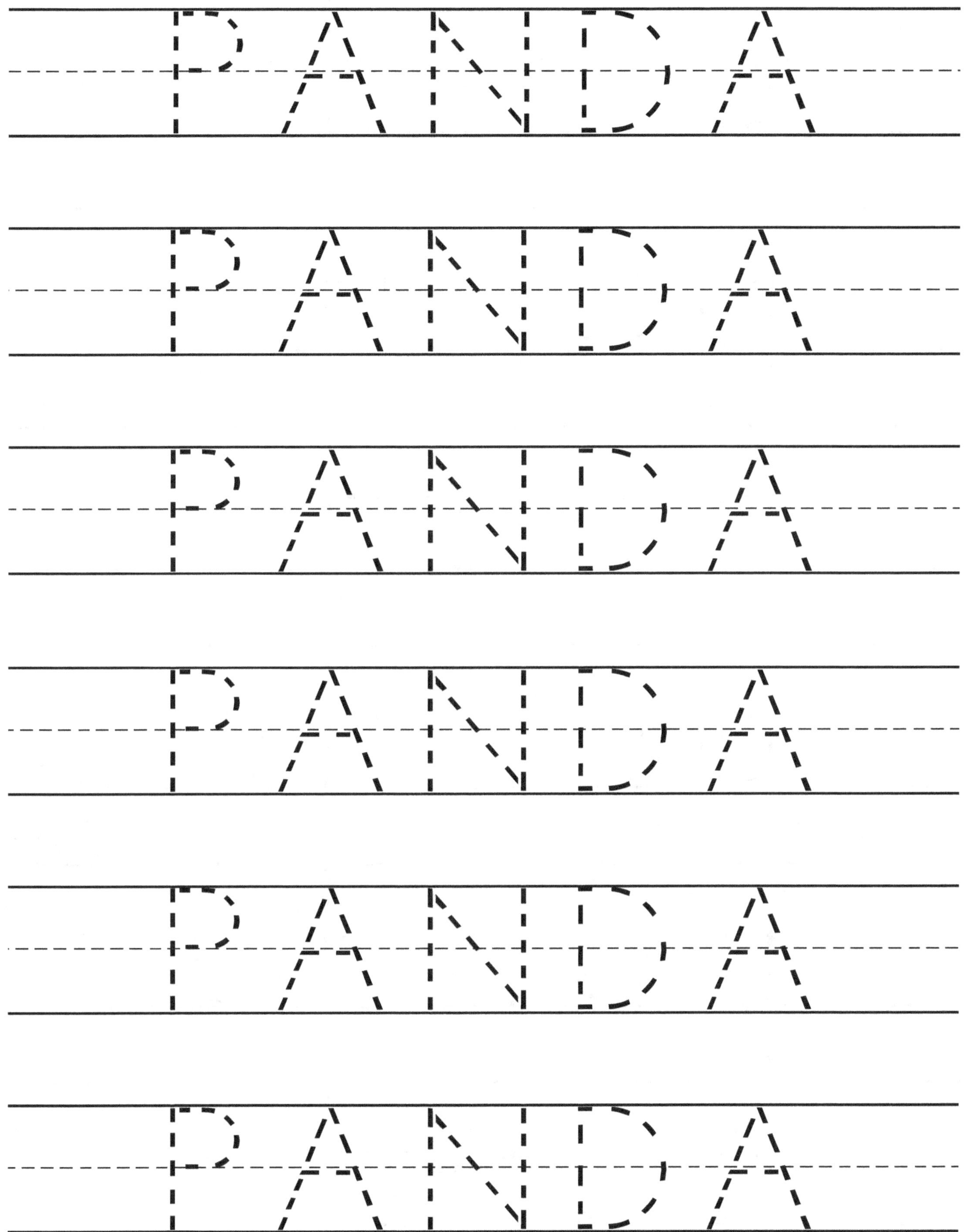

panda

panda

panda

panda

panda

panda

Q is for

quail

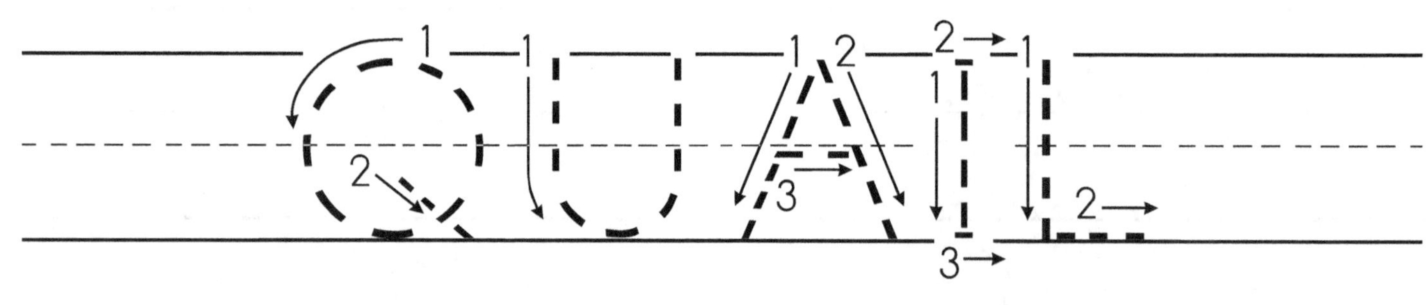

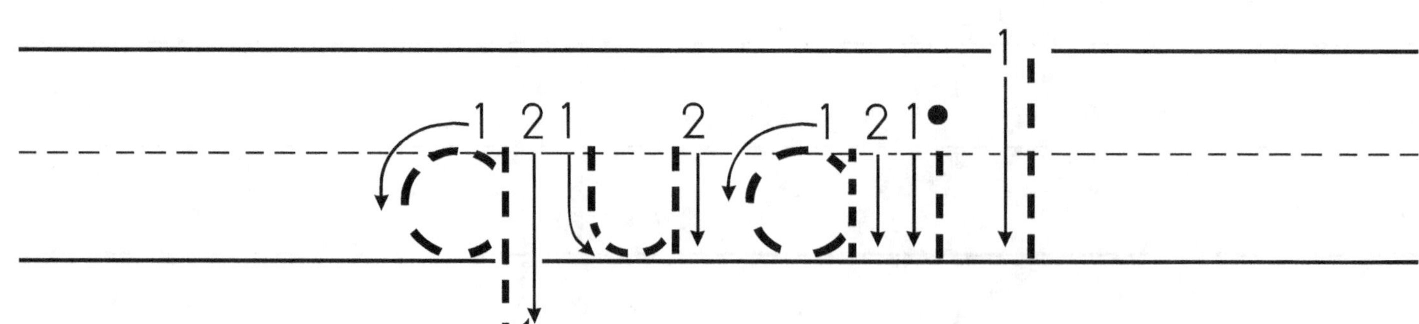

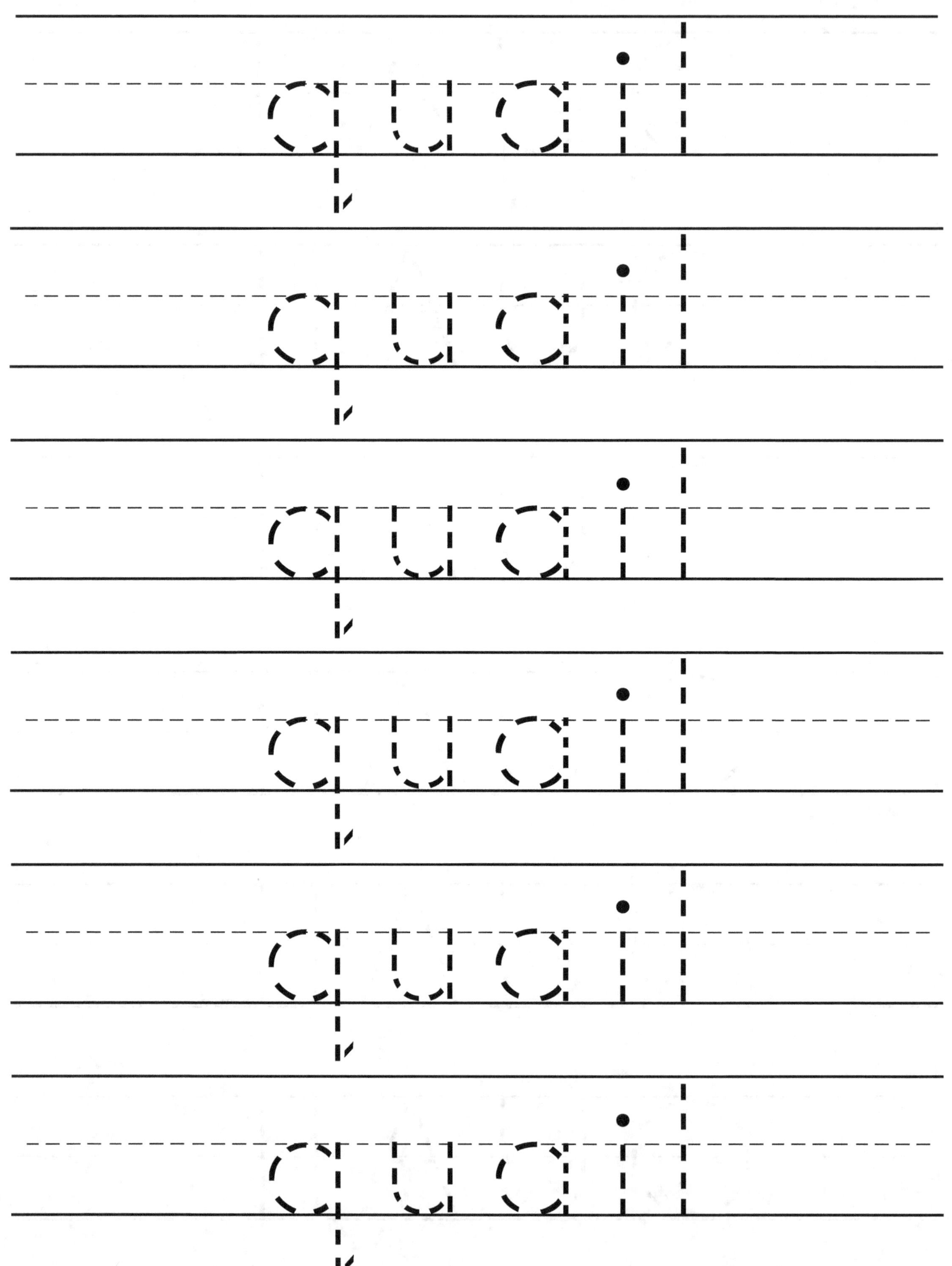

R is for

raccoon

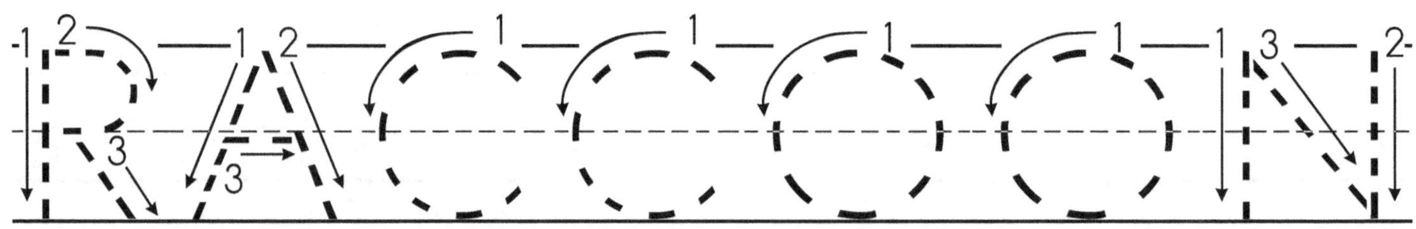

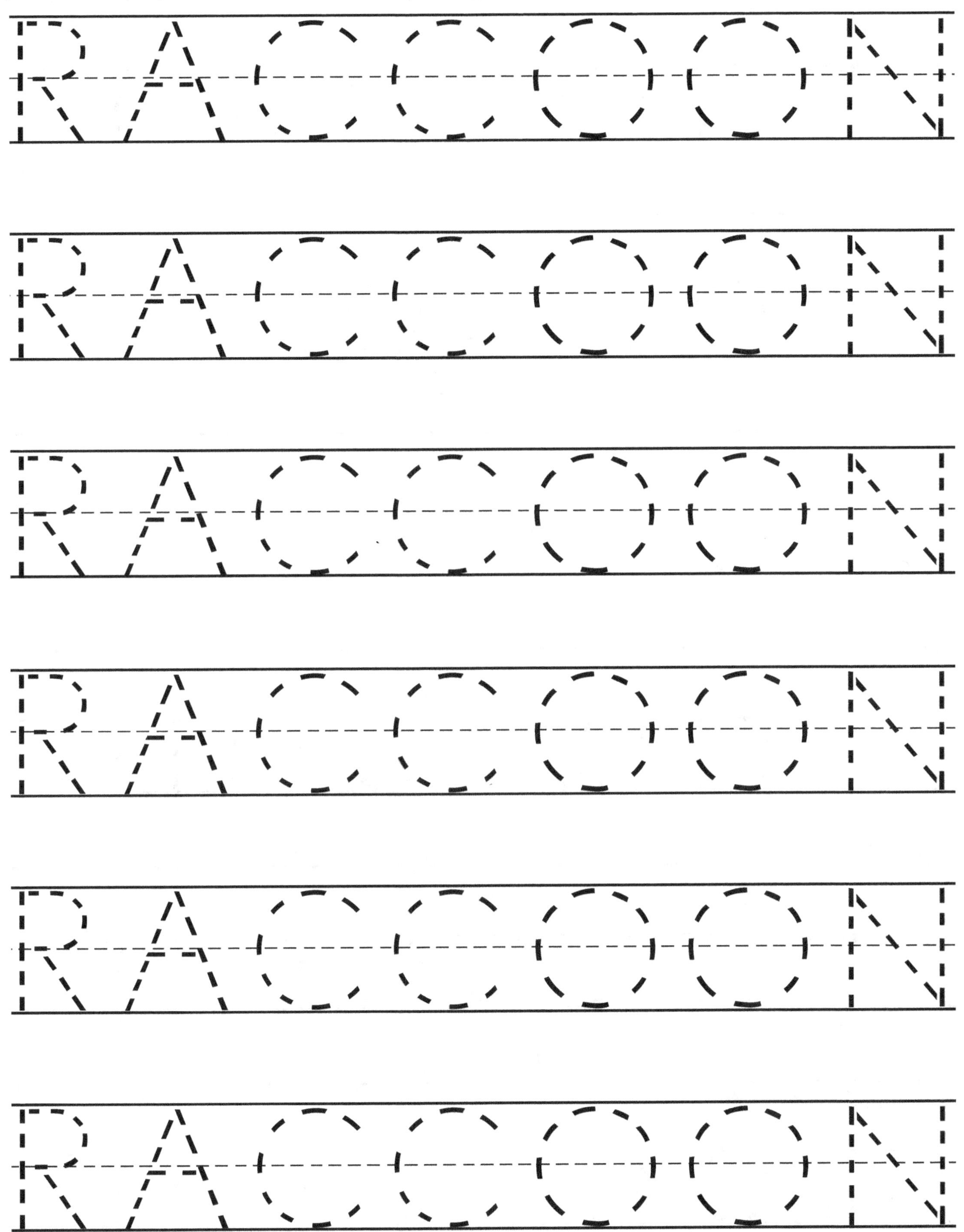

RACCOON
RACCOON
RACCOON
RACCOON
RACCOON
RACCOON

raccoon

raccoon

raccoon

raccoon

raccoon

raccoon

S is for

squirrel

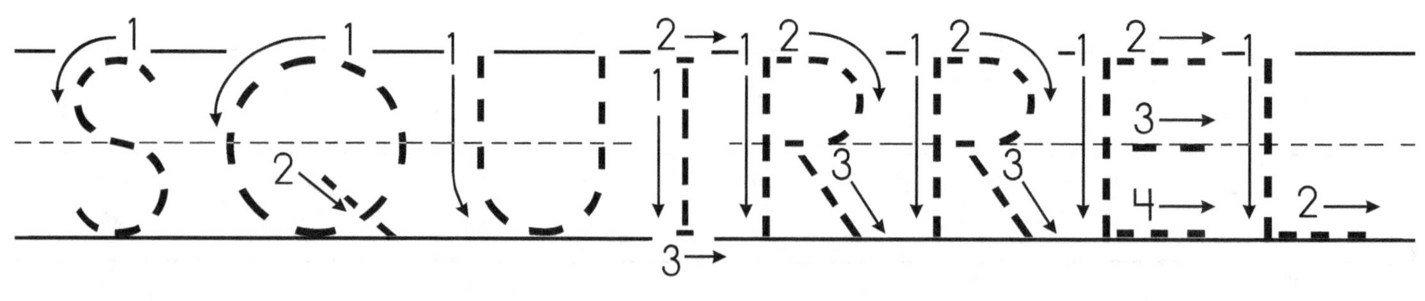

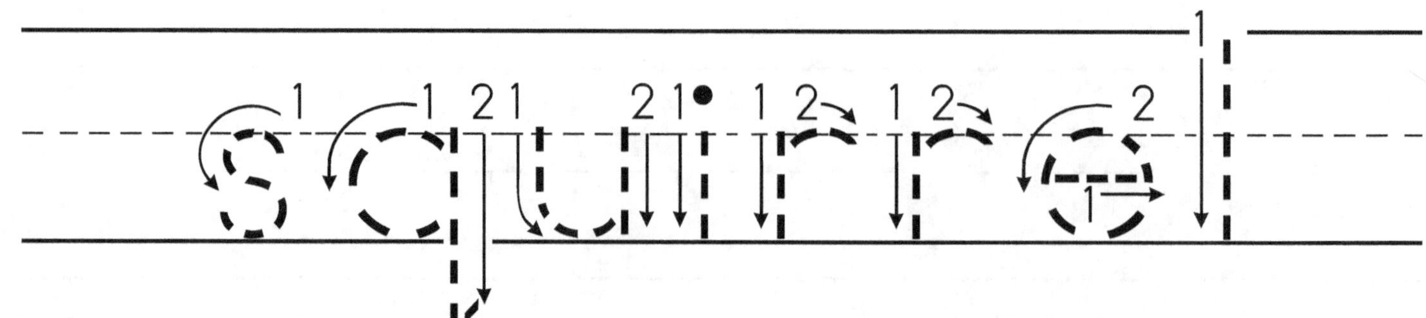

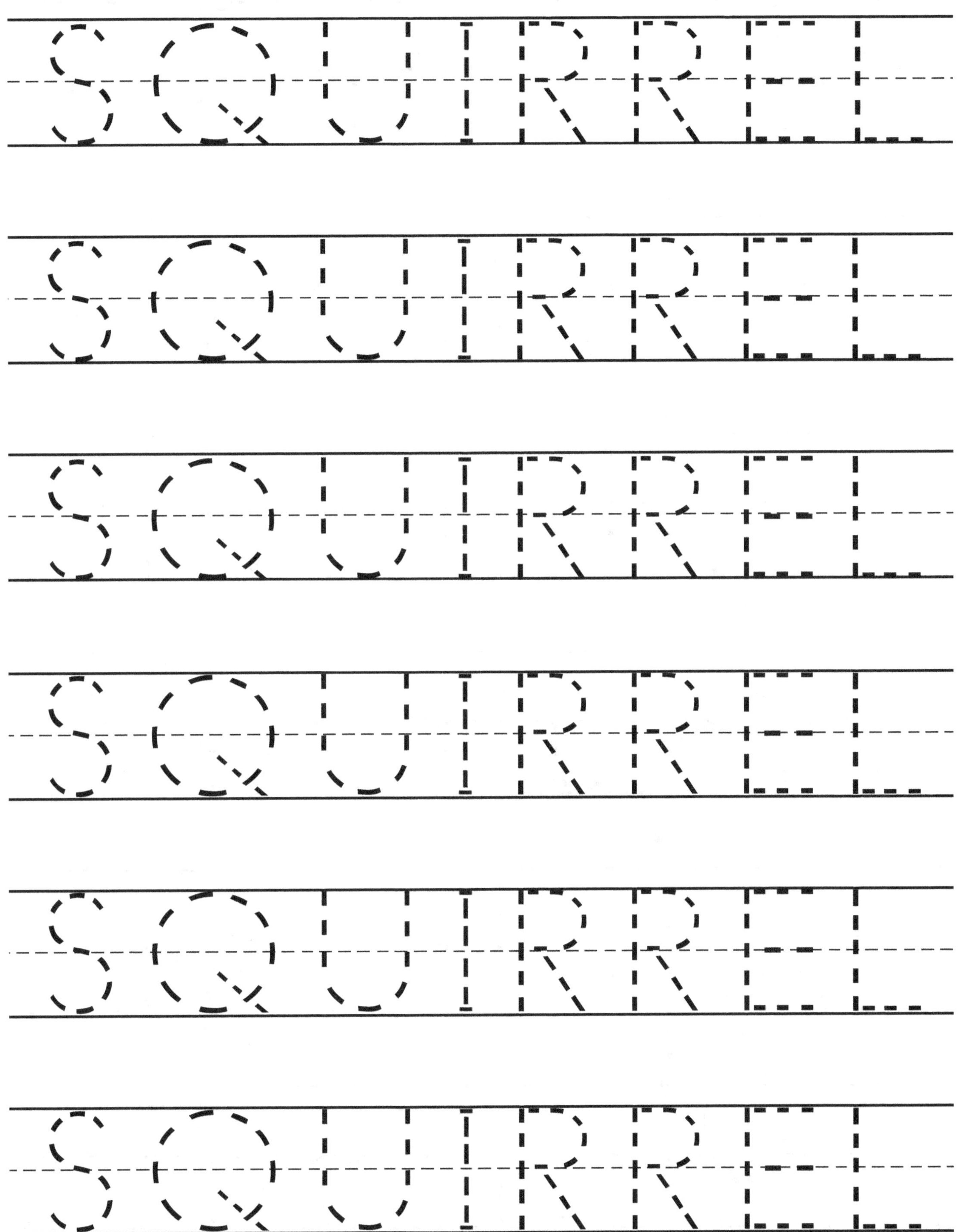

SQUIRREL
SQUIRREL
SQUIRREL
SQUIRREL
SQUIRREL
SQUIRREL

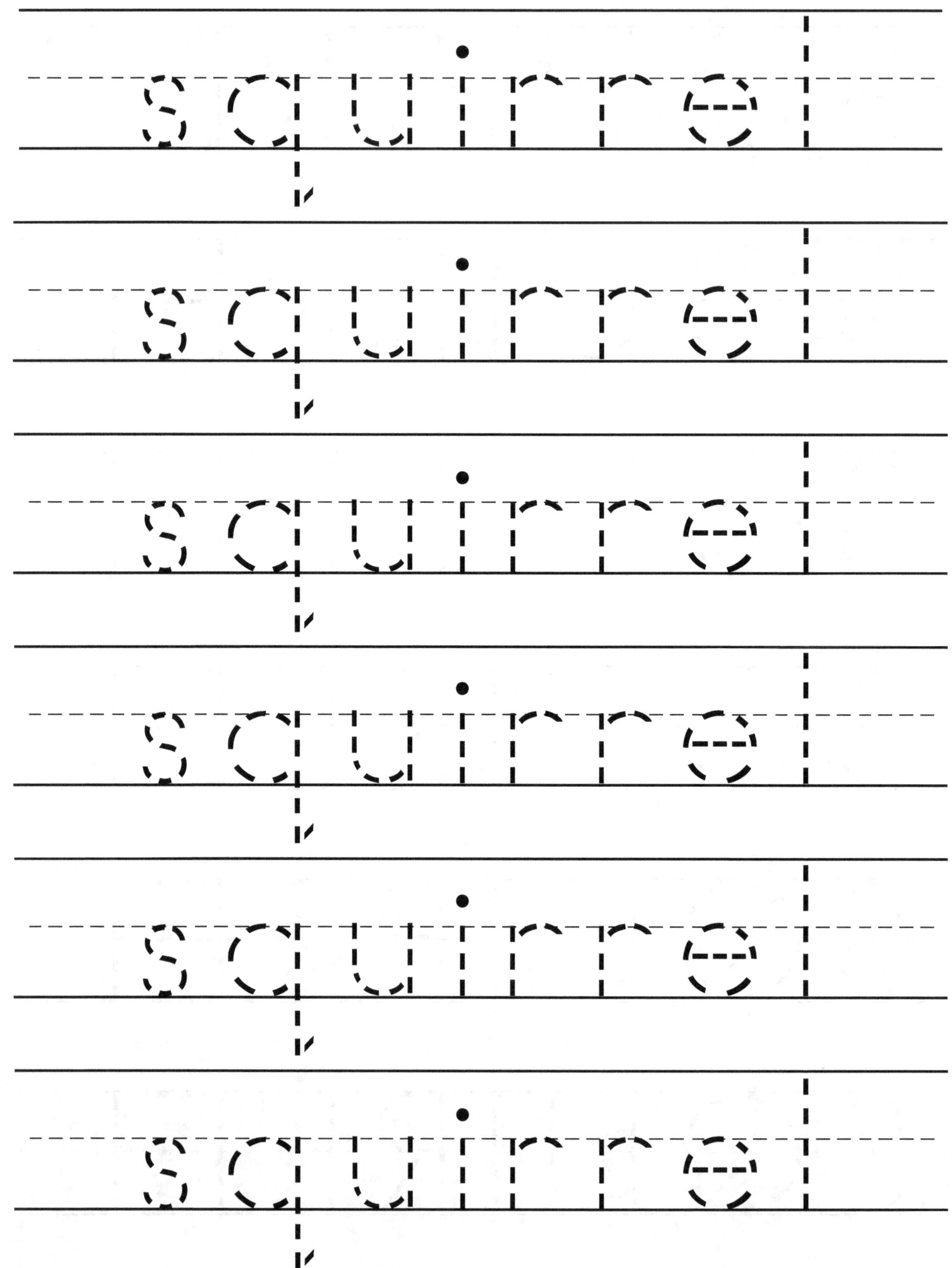

squirrel
squirrel
squirrel
squirrel
squirrel
squirrel

T is for

turtle

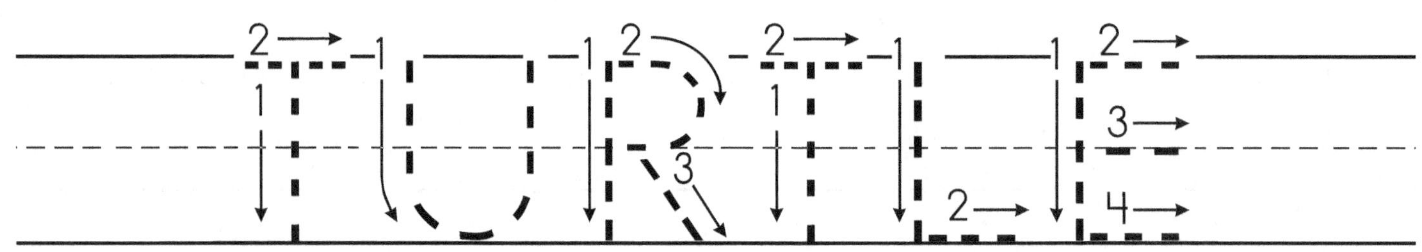

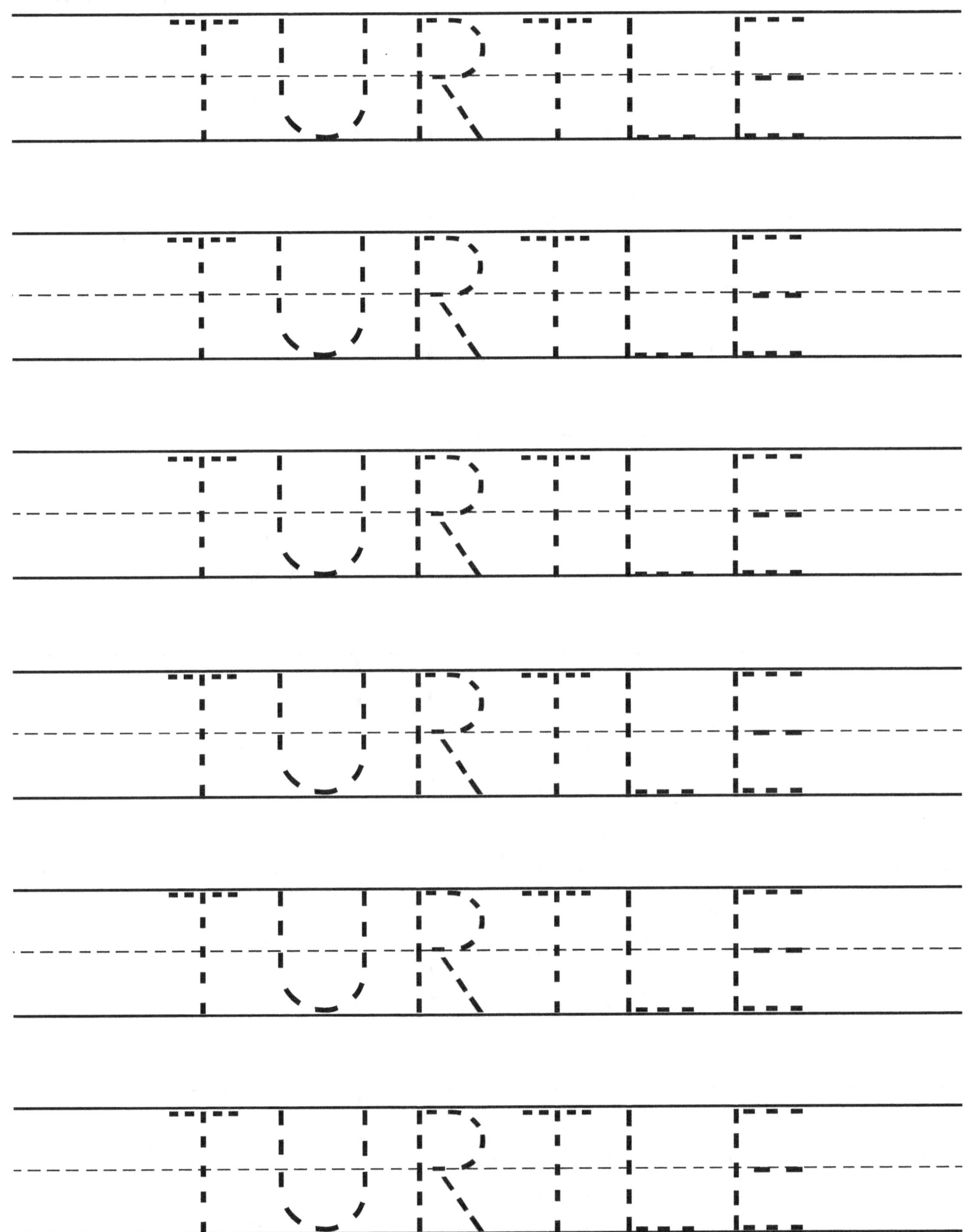
TURTLE
TURTLE
TURTLE
TURTLE
TURTLE
TURTLE

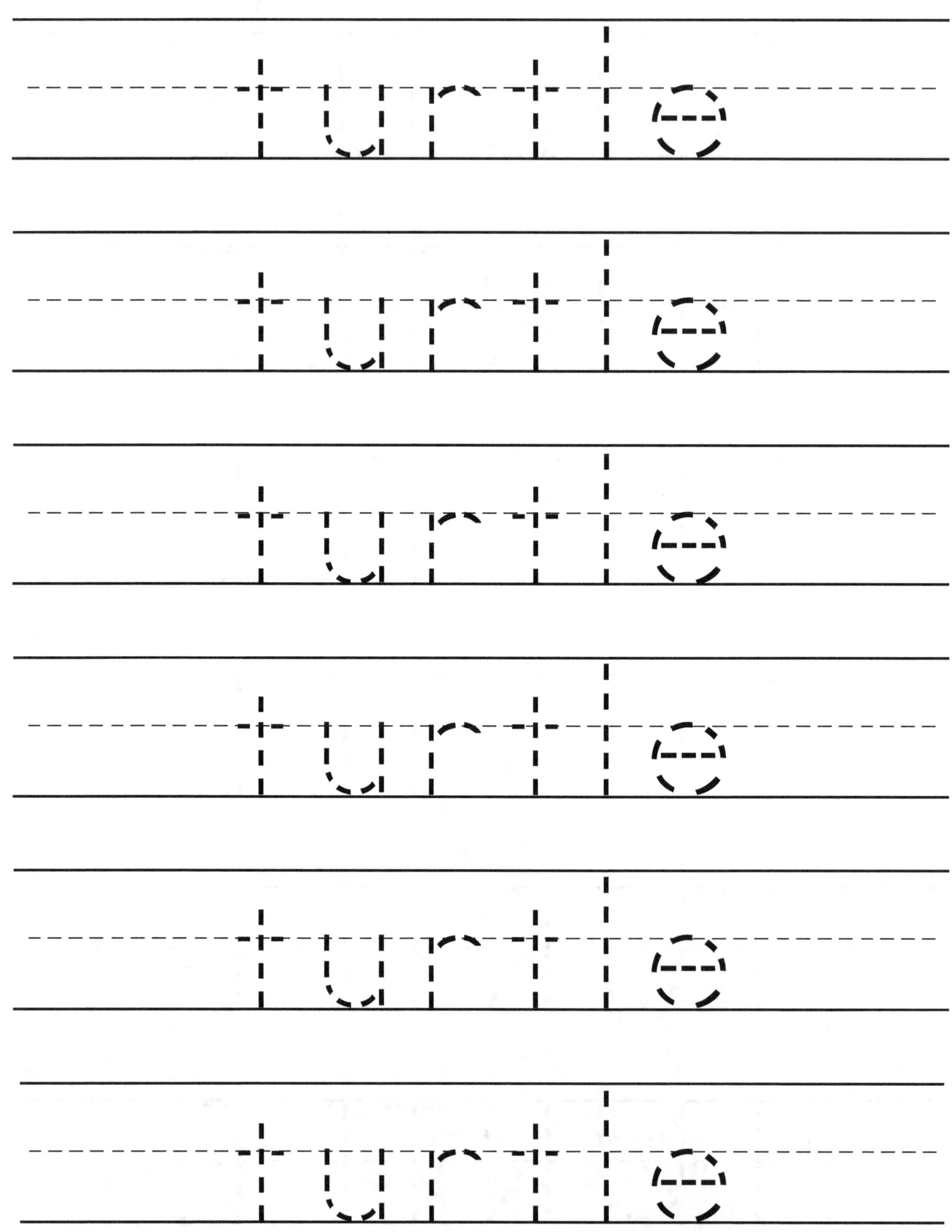

U is for

unicorn

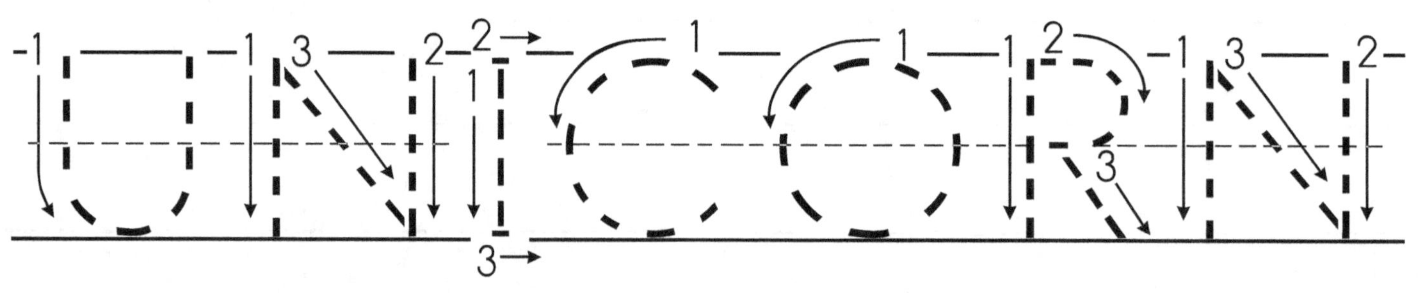

UNICORN
UNICORN
UNICORN
UNICORN
UNICORN
UNICORN

V is for

vulture

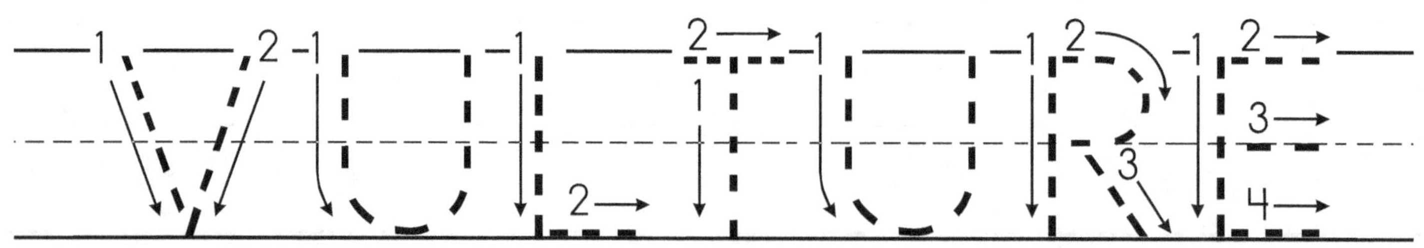

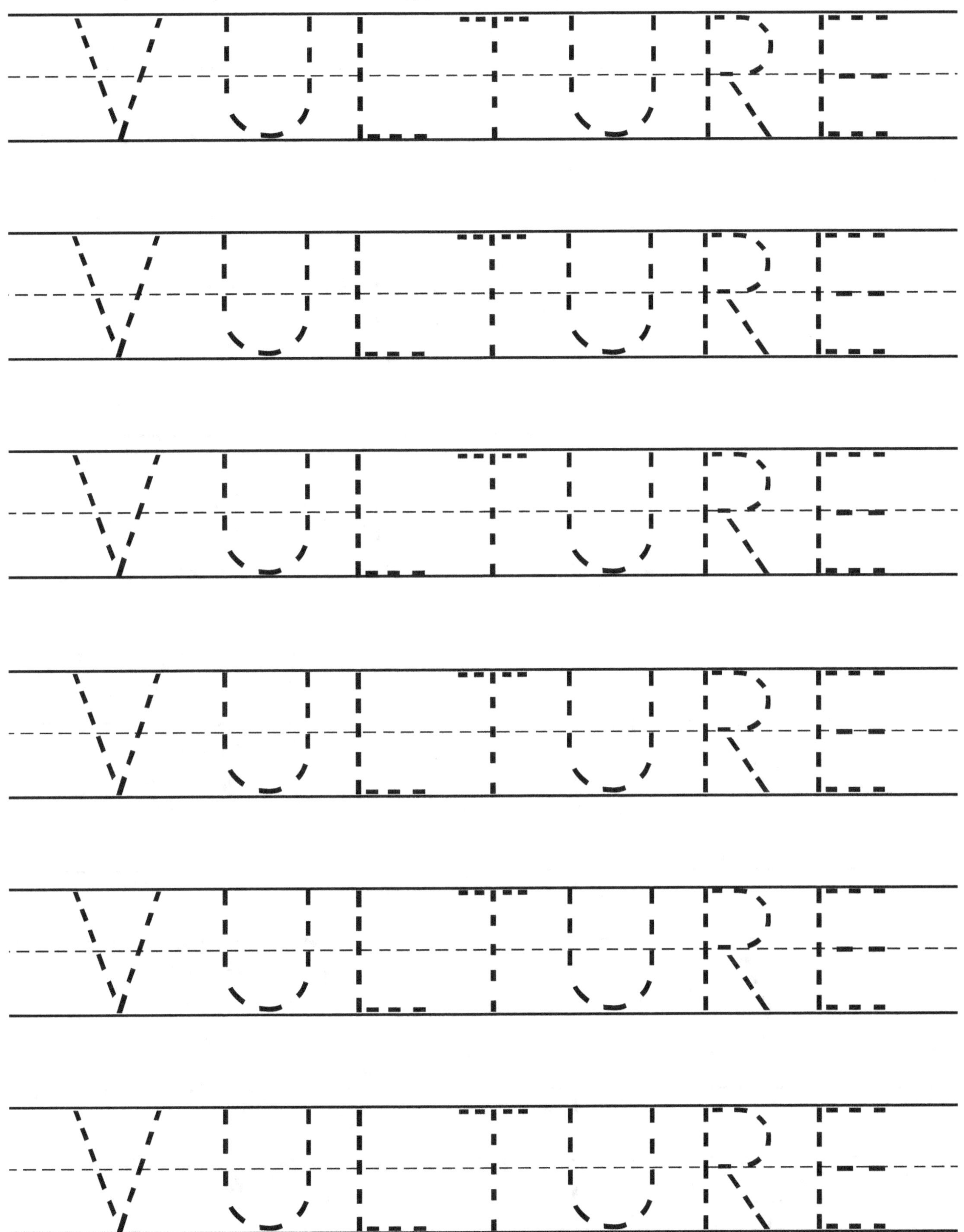

VULTURE
VULTURE
VULTURE
VULTURE
VULTURE
VULTURE

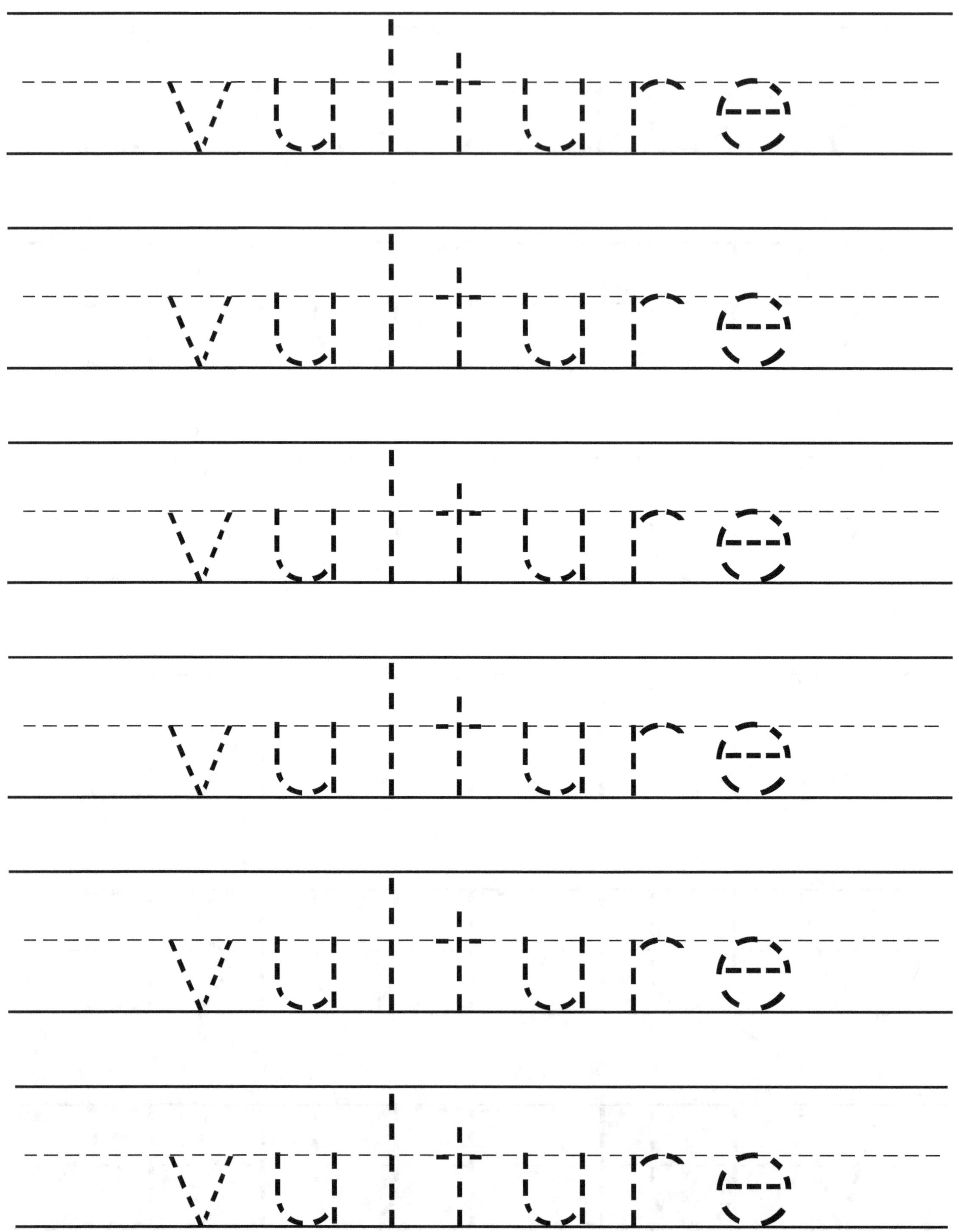

W is for

W

wolf

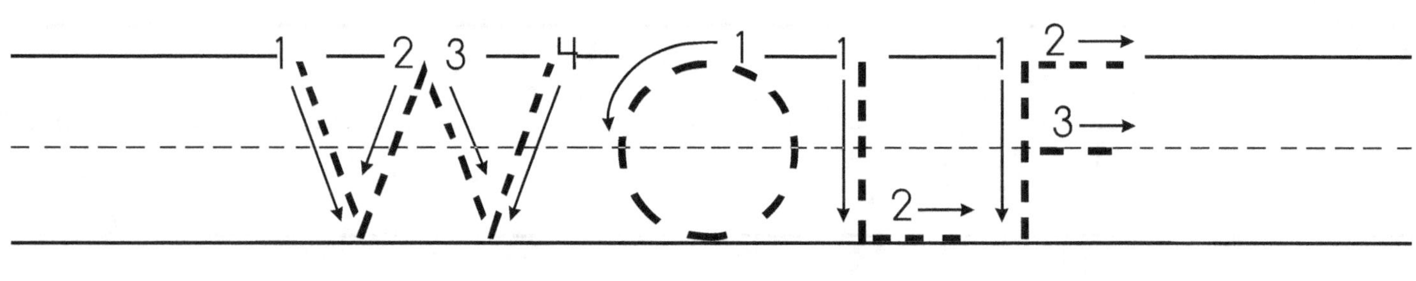

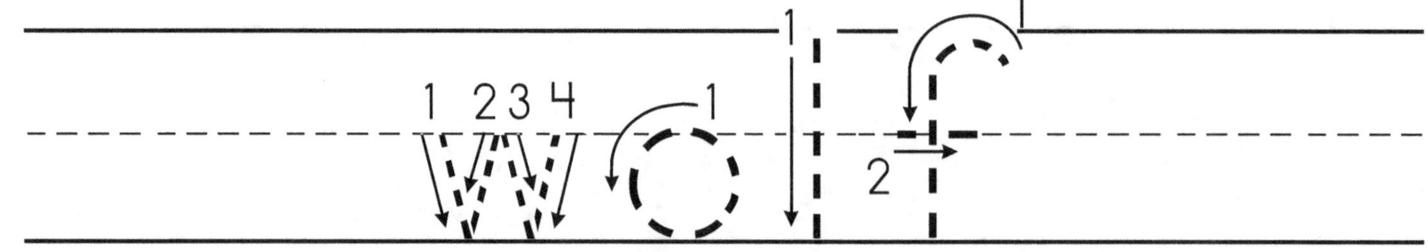

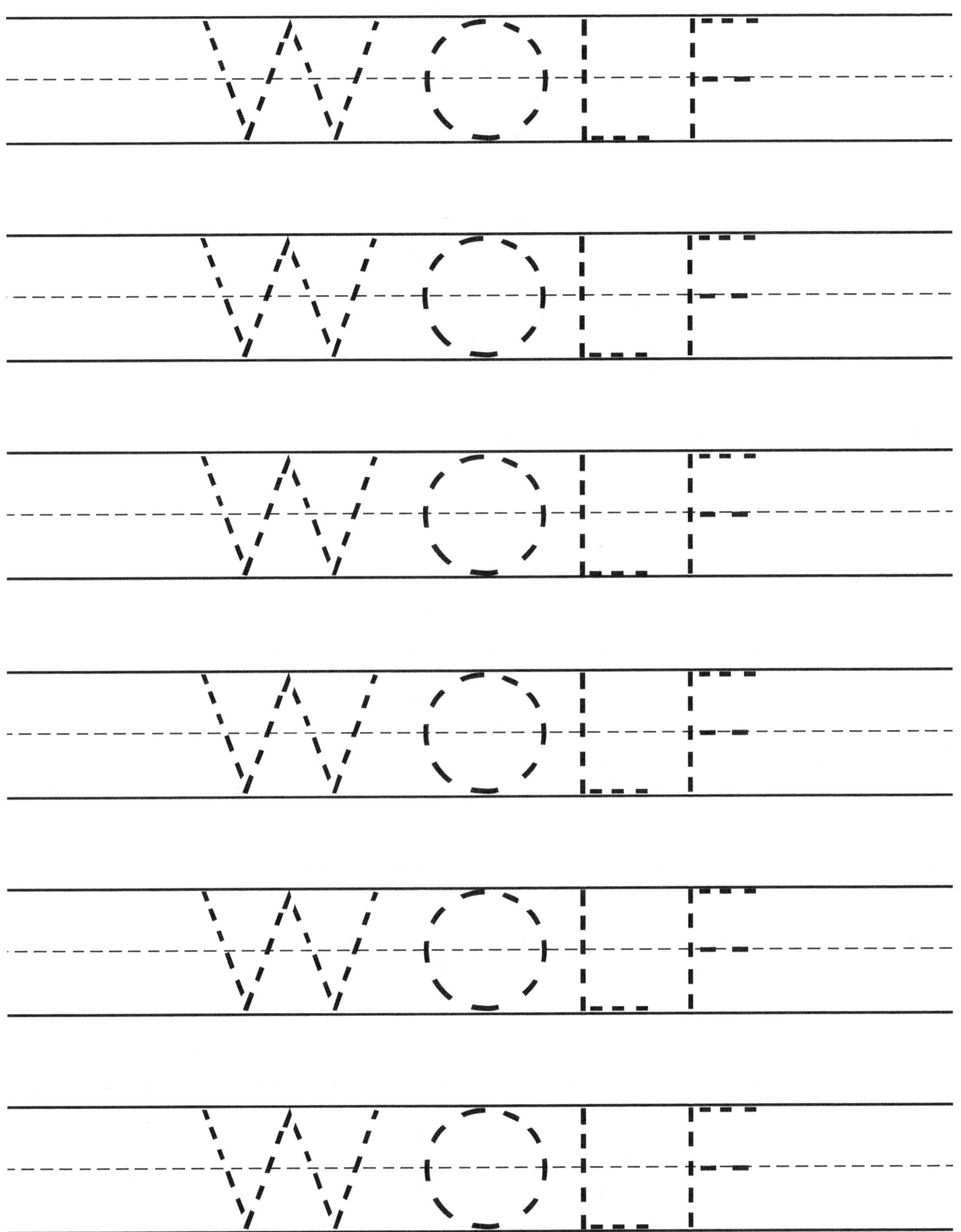

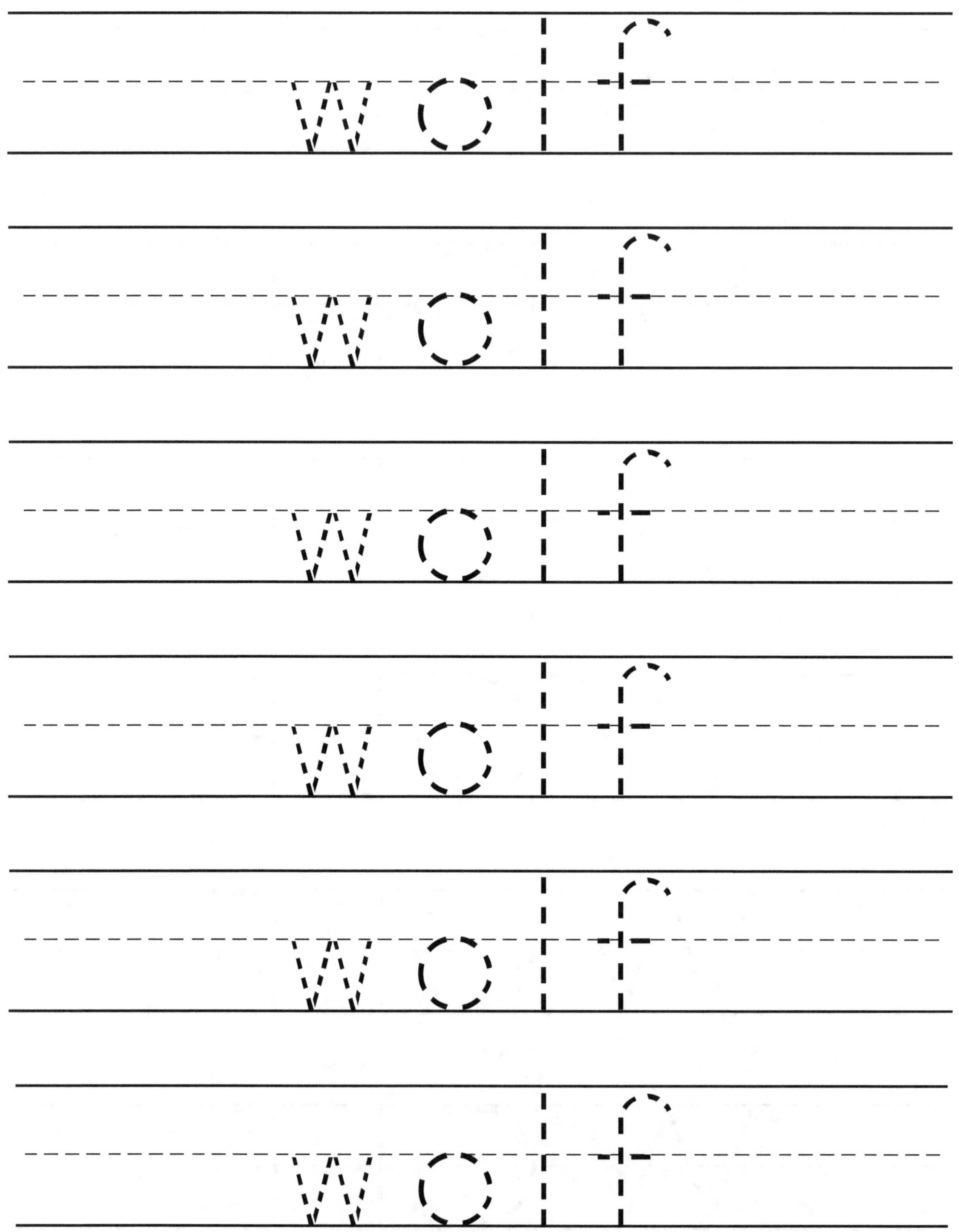

X is for

x-ray fish

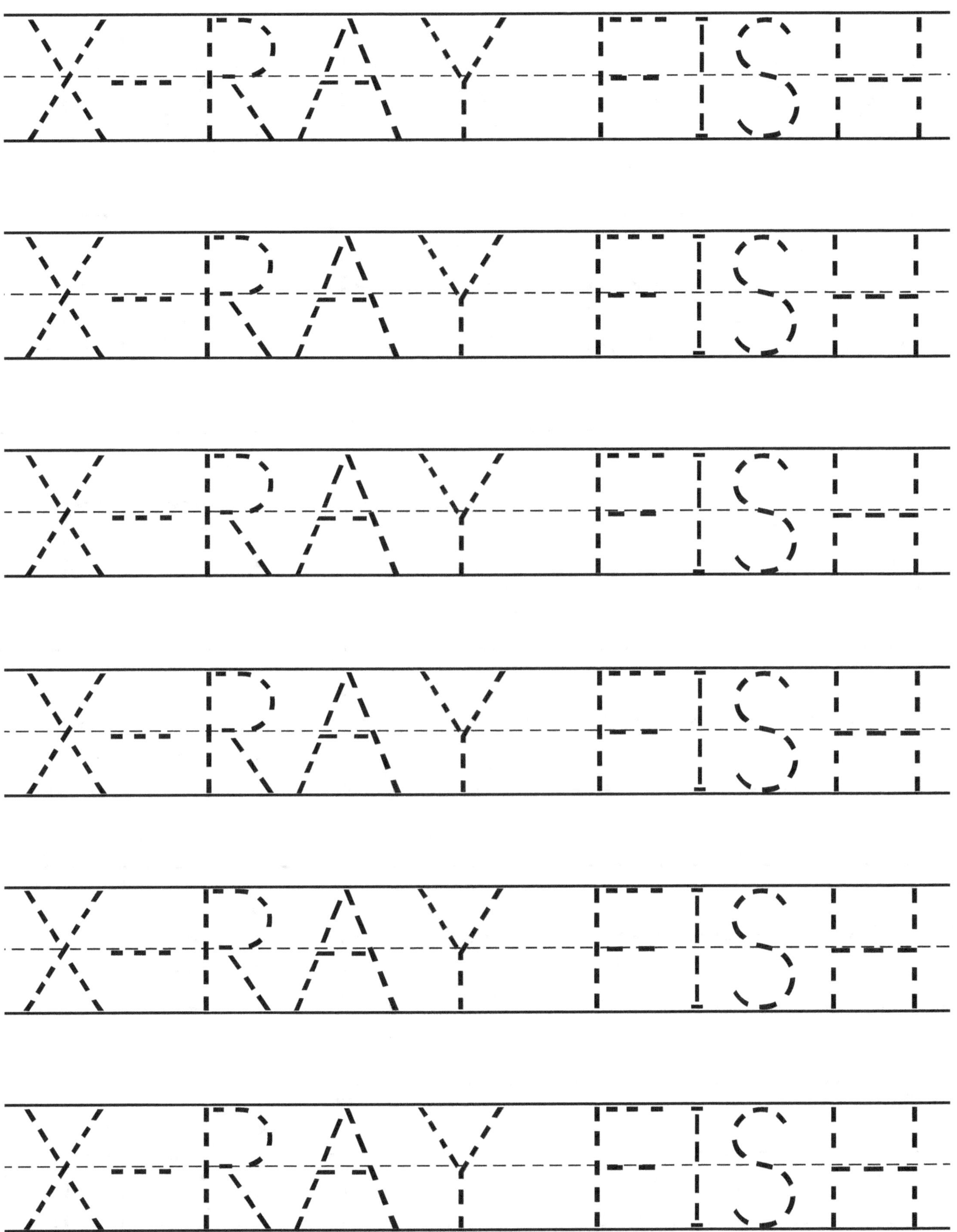

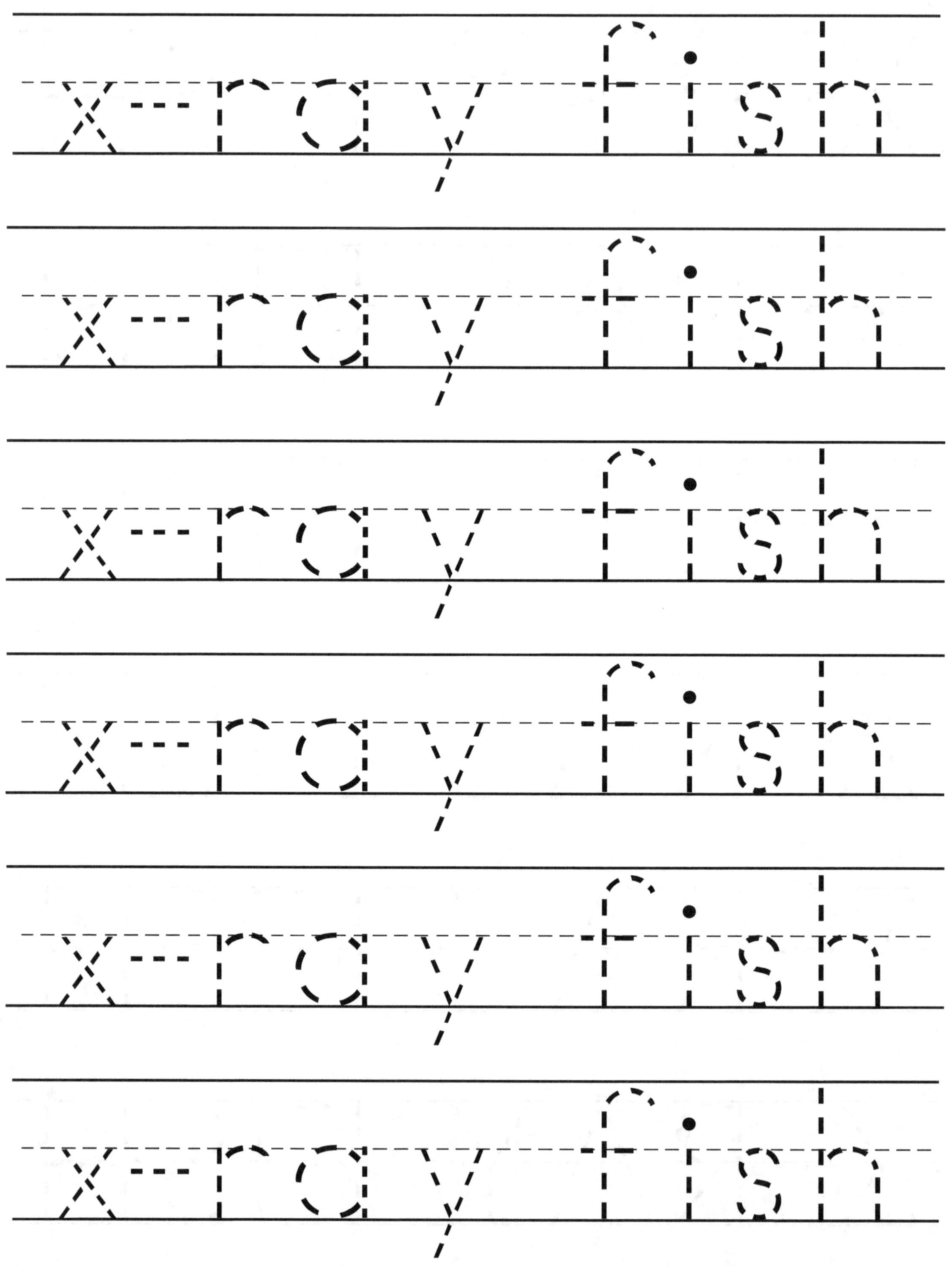
x-ray fish
x-ray fish
x-ray fish
x-ray fish
x-ray fish
x-ray fish

Y is for

yak

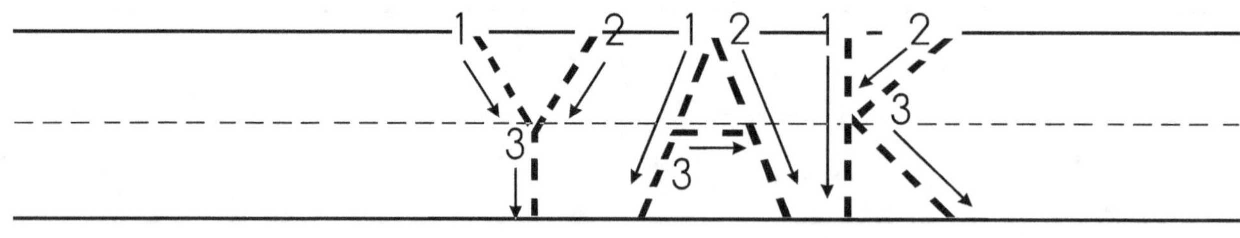

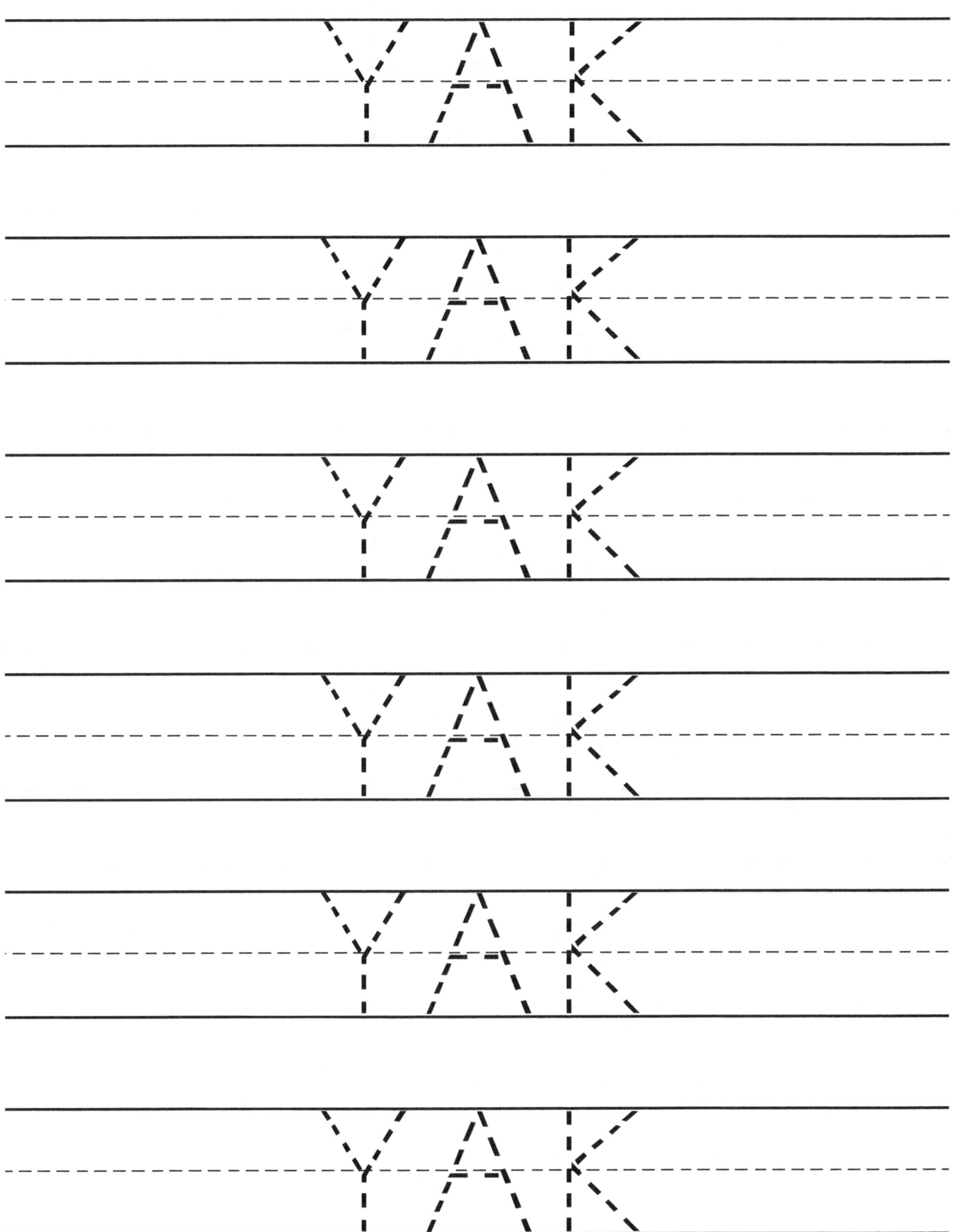

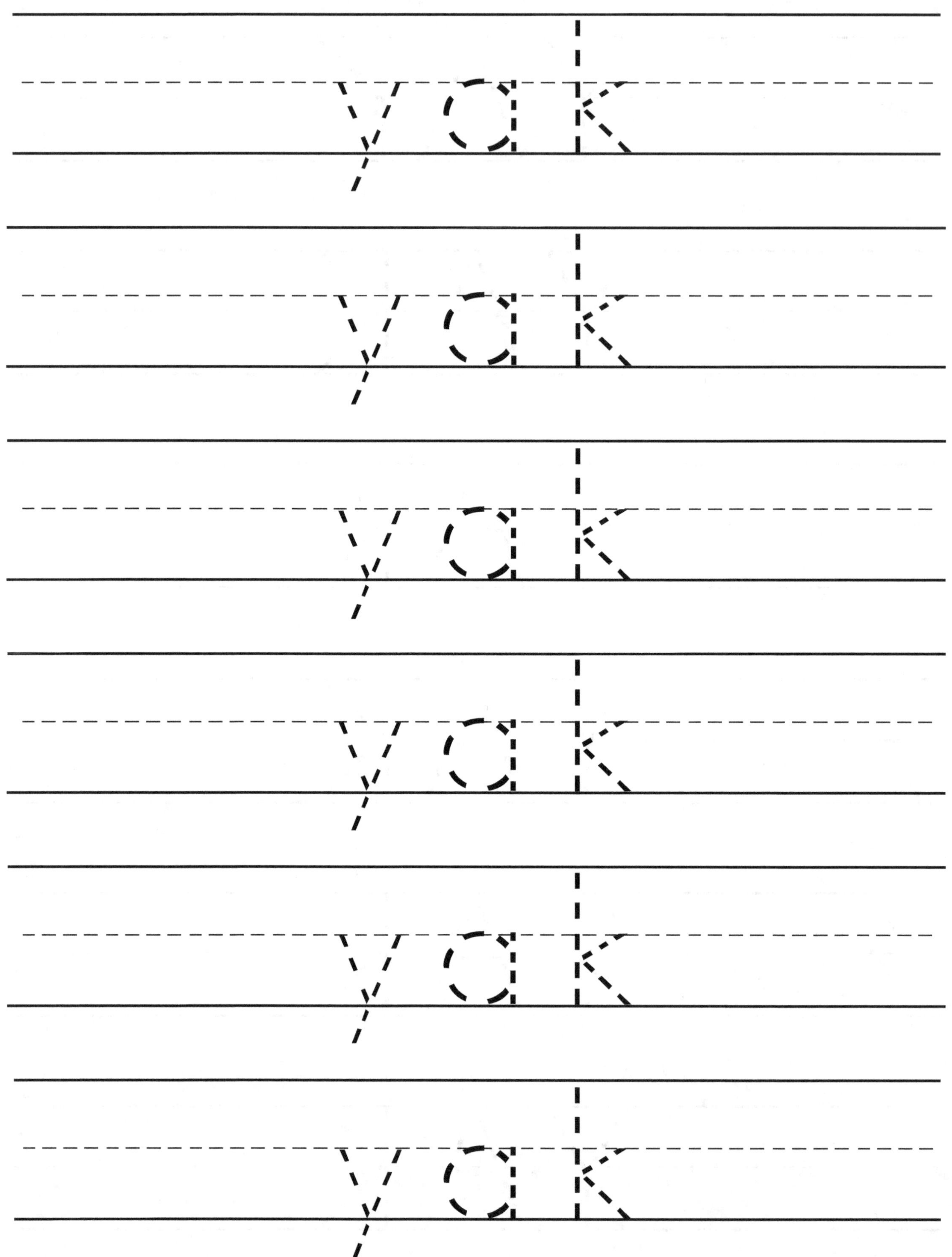

Z is for

zebra

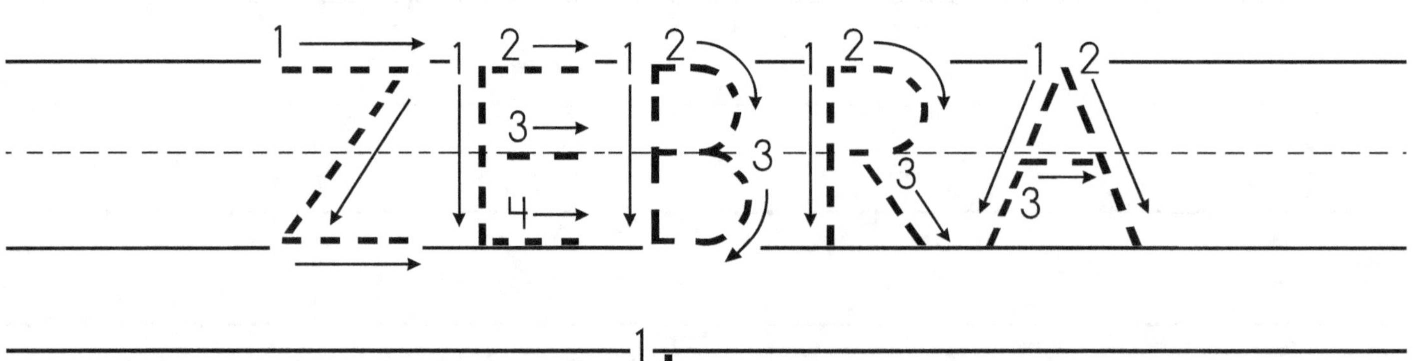

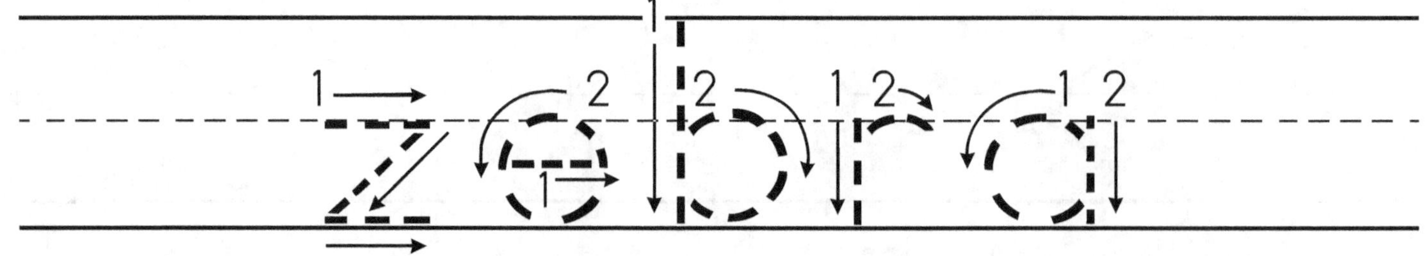

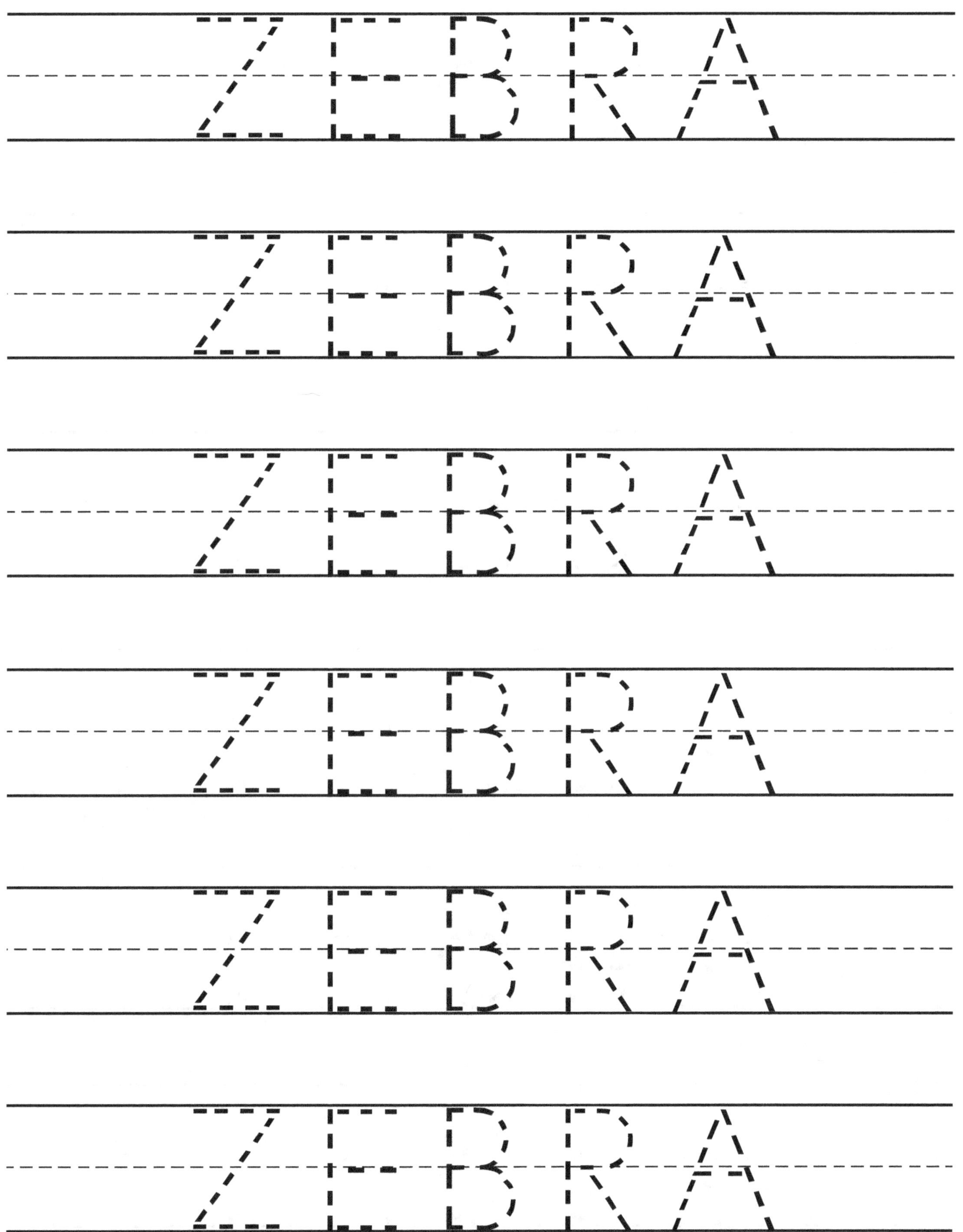

zebra

zebra

zebra

zebra

zebra

zebra

Practice

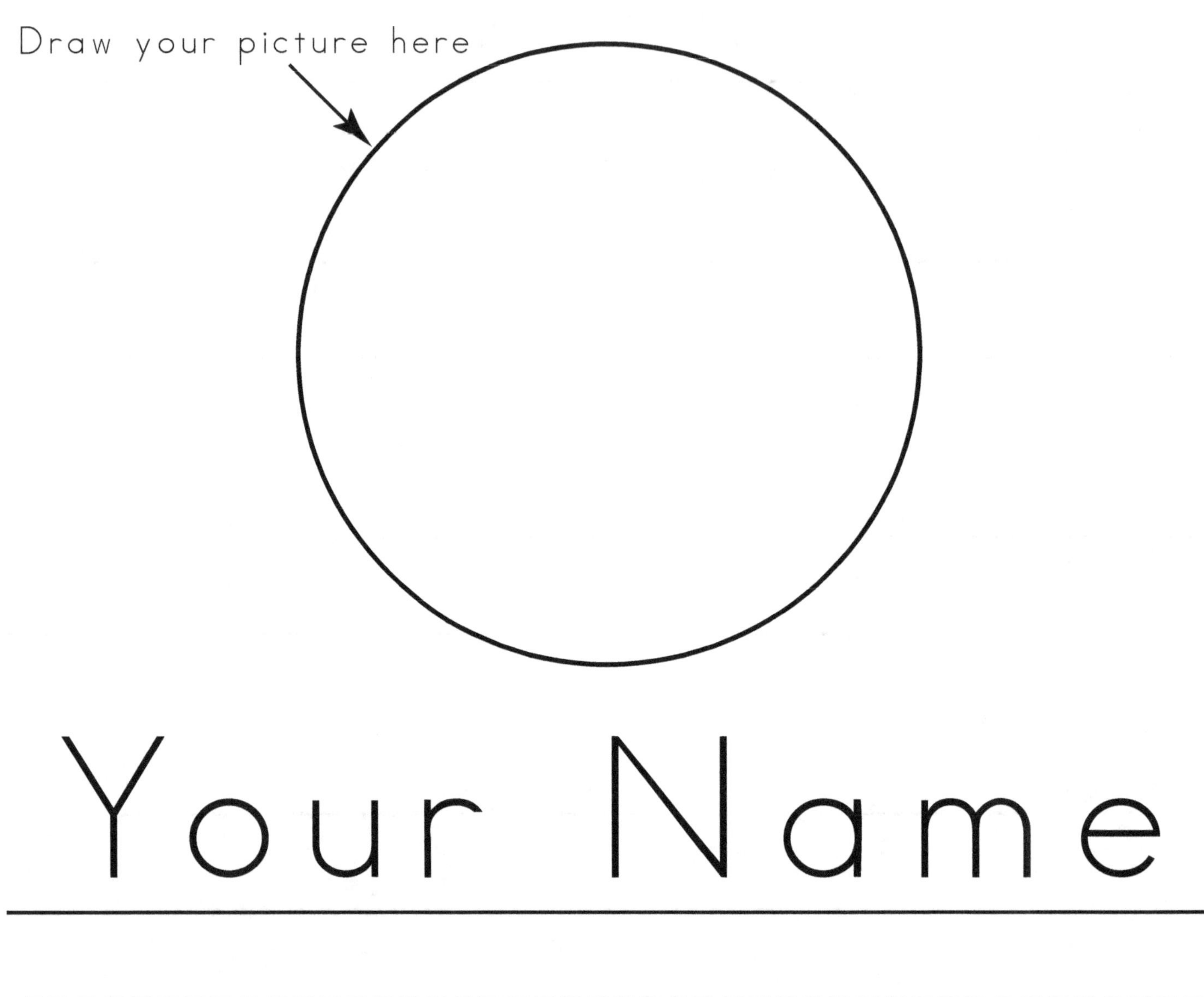

Your Name

About the Author

Talia Knight is the pen name of the author/artist. She is a prolific reader, and when she was faced with the task of choosing a pen name, she knew just where to turn. She chose "Talia" because it's the name of one her favorite fantasy heroines, and "Knight" because she loves sword and sorcery fantasy.

Of course, once she had the name, she had to create a picture worthy of her new fantasy-inspired alter ego. What could be more appropriate than a strong female (she has to be strong—she's wearing all that armor!) trekking through the desert with perfect hair and absolutely no sweat dripping down her face? Her makeup isn't even smudged. Realistically, she ought to be laid out flat on that sand, red as a lobster with heatstroke.

On a more serious note, Talia considers herself the luckiest person in the world because she has the privilege of helping to care for her handicapped sister while living in the great state of Texas. When she's not spending time with her sister or playing with her many nieces and nephews, she's usually doing something with books. Creating, writing, editing, selling—you name it, she's probably done it.

Want FREE coloring pages?

Talia Knight is giving away a free coloring book

If you like <u>FREE</u>, you can download your coloring book here:

TranquilityColoring.com/harmony

www.ingramcontent.com/pod-product-compliance
Lightning Source LLC
Chambersburg PA
CBHW081309250726
48662CB00008B/2467